Bumming with the FURIES

Out on the Trail of Experience

Peter M. Leschak

Illustrated by
Mark Coyle
Fred Yiran
Patrick Dwyer

North Star Press of St. Cloud, Inc.

Credits:

"The Young Barbarians," *Minnesota Monthly*, Vol. 20, No. 7, July 1986.

"Open Pit Playground," *Minnesota Monthly*, Vol. 18, No. 9, September 1984.

"A .44 Magnum Manifesto" (under the title, "A Back-Road Horror Ride"), *New York Times Magazine*, March 4, 1990.

"Out for Blood," *Mpls./St. Paul*, Vol. 14, No. 10, October 1986.

"The 8-Sweep," *Twin Cities*, Vol. 11, No. 7, July 1988.

"Quarterback Keeper," *Mpls./St. Paul*, Vol. 17, No. 11, November 1989.

"A Passage and a Parachute" (under the title "The Fall"), *TWA Ambassador*, September 1986.

"Seeing the Elephant," *New Age Journal*, Vol. 2, No. 4, 1985; and (under the title, "Facing the Elephant"), *Backpacker*, Vol. 18, No. 2, April 1990.

"The Seven Golden Cheetahs," *Twin Cities*, Vol. 11, No. 9, September 1988, and *Runner's World*, Vol. 25, No. 10, October 1990.

"Cannon Fodder," *Men's Health*, Vol. 5, No. 5, December 1990.

"Rainy Night at the Sewage Plant" (in part), *Minnesota Monthly*, Vol. 19, No. 9, September 1985.

"Midway Road," *Mpls/St. Paul*, Vol 14, No. 2, February 1986; and *Minneapolis Star and Tribune Sunday Magazine*, July 16, 1989.

"Free Beer and Destiny," *Writer's Digest*, Vol. 70, No. 1, January 1989.

Library of Congress Cataloging-in-Publication Data

Leschak, Peter M., 1951-
    Bumming with the furies : out on the trail of experience / Peter M. Leschak ; illustrated by Mark Coyle, Fred Yiran, Patrick Dwyer.
    200 p. 23 cm.
    ISBN 0-87839-078-2 : $9.95
    1. Leschak, Peter M., 1951-   . 2. Minnesota—Biography.
    3. Minnesota—Social life and customs.   I. Title.
    F610.L49   1993
977.6'033'092--dc20
[B]
                                                      93-7993
                                                        CIP

Printed in the United States of America by Versa Press of East Peoria, Illinois.
Published by: North Star Press of St. Cloud, Inc.
                       P.O. Box 451
                       St. Cloud, Minnesota 56302

In memory of
John Curtis Niemi
1951-1975
It was too short a journey.

Acknowledgements

I am grateful to Corinne and Rita Dwyer of North Star Press for their suggestions and editing and for the general input that refined this book. I also thank all the magazine editors who gave some of this material its first chance—especially Claude Peck, Jeff Johnson, Sylvia Paine, Eric Copage, Doug Tice and Lisbet Nilson.

Contents

Bumming with the Furies

"Tut, tut, child," said the Duchess.
"Everything's got a moral if only you can find it."

Lewis Carroll,
Alice's Adventures in Wonderland

Introduction

I topped a rise at about fifty miles per hour and encountered a big green Buick pulled over on the left shoulder but pointed in the direction I was traveling. That was odd, and I slowed down. The January afternoon was cold, so I could see the Buick was idling—spewing out heavy, dark exhaust. The car was parked in front of a rural mailbox, and I guessed the driver was checking his mail. On the right was a driveway.

I was almost abreast of the Buick when it spun off the shoulder, crossed the left lane and surged directly in front of me, apparently shooting for the driveway.

I mashed down the brake pedal of my half-ton pickup—stomped it to the firewall. But through a jolt of adrenaline and white-knuckled fear hurtled the lucid realization that collision was unavoidable. When he whipped into my lane we were less than twenty feet apart.

The highway was icy and my truck fishtailed as it skidded into the passenger side of the car. The impact shoved me up onto the steering wheel, and it seemed as if I lifted the Buick as I crushed its front door and kept on going. The window glass blew apart, and through the opening I could clearly see the driver—he was ricochet-

1

ing inside the car, loose and limp like a rag doll. I saw his head bounce off the roof, the steering wheel, the headrest. Locked together in a screeching metal grip, my momentum carried us off the highway, across the shoulder and down into the ditch.

We stopped, and I sat for a moment, still latched onto the steering wheel. My engine had died, and I shut off the key. I didn't seem to be hurt. Trembling a little, I tried to open the door, but it was jammed. I squeezed past the floor shift lever and tried the passenger door; it creaked open, and I stumbled out into the snow. I was afraid of what I'd find in the Buick.

The entire passenger side of the car was caved in, but the engine was running. In fact, it was being revved, and the rear tires were spinning impotently in the snow. I hurried to the driver's side and jerked open the door.

The driver seemed young, and his face was bruised and bloody, punctured in several places by tiny shards of glass. It was ugly, but not serious. He was dazed and seemed stoned or drunk. (He later told police he'd been turning into his own driveway—in a town *twenty-five miles* away.) He was oblivious to the magnitude of the accident and was trying to power his way back onto the highway. After the obligatory, "Are you okay?" to which I got no response (and which instantly sounded ridiculous since he obviously wasn't okay), I grabbed his arm and said, "Look!" I pointed to the exposed radiator of my truck, which was nestled into his front seat. "You're not going anywhere." I reached over, switched off his ignition and slipped the keys into his jacket pocket. I helped him out of the car, and he stared in disbelief at the wreckage.

He swayed a little in the ditch, dripping blood into the snow and chanting, "Oh, damn! Oh, damn! Oh, damn!" in a stunned, whining litany.

By then I was angry and broke into his shocked reverie to demand what the hell he'd been doing. He didn't know. The person whose driveway it was ran out to the road, and I asked her to call an ambulance. I brushed the glass off the front seat of the Buick and helped the kid (he looked like a teenager) back inside to wait for the medics.

I leaned against the Buick and ruefully considered my truck. It looked like the end of the road and the beginning of an expensive hassle. First there'd be the sheriff and a wrecker, then insurance adjustors and body men, and then in this case, it turned out, a municipal judge. In a fairer world I would have had the option of trading the whole mess for a rousing case of food poisoning or a severe hangover. On the other hand, if conditions had been a little different (dry road, higher speed), I could've been maimed or killed. Options forge a two-edged sword.

In retrospect, the crash seemed ineluctable, foreordained. Move by move, throughout the day, our respective plans, timing, and trajectories had led to this dramatic meeting. There had been a precise sequence of events. If the least had been altered, the outcome would have been different. For example, a half-hour before, I had stopped at the store to buy a few things. If I had picked out just one more item, I would have needed a few more seconds to decide between brands, used a few more seconds to take the extra item off shelf, and the clerk would have taken a moment to ring it up and drop it in the bag. Added up, it could have been enough seconds for the Buick to rip across the road *behind* me rather than in front of me. If I had been in the mood for a candy bar, or browsed for a magazine, or exchanged three more sentences of small talk with the clerk, there would have been no collision.

But those were potential events of the past several minutes; what about the past several years? I could have made any number of decisions and choices in life that would have put me not only on another road, but in another state, or even another country. Hell, I could already have been dead for ten years, and the Buick would've had the road to itself.

When I was still in junior high school, our parish priest had drawn me aside one day and asked if I would like to be enrolled in a seminary. He thought the "vocation of the priesthood" might be appropriate for me, and the Church began indoctrination early.

I was a "good boy." I was polite to adults and generally did as I was told. I was religious, earned good grades in catechism class, and didn't antagonize the nuns. But the seminary? I said, "No" immediately. I surprised myself with the instant certainty of my reply—especially to a priest. The robed men represented Authority—they were at the apex of a pyramid of elders. To just say, "No," not even tactfully demuring with, "I'll think about it," was shocking; but I did it. It was a "road not taken," and how different my life would have been: a dogmatized celibate, who probably never owned a pickup.

In that light, if this accident was one of the consequences of spurning the seminary, I guess it was a small price to pay. In a twisted sort of way I could even be grateful. But for the rest of the day I was haunted by the notion of the *unavoidable*.

"Thou art," wrote John Donne (a priest), "slave to fate, chance, kings, and desperate men." No matter how many unilateral decisions we make, they are never made in a vacuum. There are thousands of other people making thousands of other decisions which will impinge upon ours—for good or ill. (I didn't *choose* to ram the Buick.) And not even an IBM PC could sort it all out.

"I want to seize fate by the throat," wrote Beethoven. A noble sentiment, one which many of us share. It would be gratifying to strangle the shade of determinism. But our efforts are skewbald at best, and ultimately fate leads everyone to an identical end—at least as far as this life is concerned.

There are countless paths decreed by fate, and by whatever grip we may have on its throat. This book explores one of those paths. It's not an autobiography as such. Though chapters are arranged more or less in chronological order, I won't be examining the minutiae of a single life. Rather, I'll cross the path at critical junctures, discover what happened and why, see what was gleaned, then move on.

The path is thirty-eight years long—about half a lifetime. It's been hazardous, offbeat, and shared with characters who'll probably end up in somebody's novel. It's the route of a young man seeking maturity, enlightenment, and adventure—one of the so-called "baby boomers"—fabricating rites of passage and trying to decipher *it all* at the same time. It's the chronicle of a quest for a philosophy of life— not explicitly stated in syllogisms, but implicitly revealed in the tales told. And there are some lively tales to tell.

To bum with the Furies is a gritty, ticklish run, and rarely smooth. My buddy, Wayne, who you'll meet later on, once offered a toast to "trails run, bombs rode, highways thumbed." There's more to living than that, of course, but while in the company of the Furies we sidled as close to simplicity as we'll ever be allowed. "It would be simple enough," wrote Jung, "if simplicity were not the most difficult of all things."

This book isn't a paean to the past—far from it—but to know who you are, you must recall who you were. And you, reader, are in here somewhere. Go ahead, take a look; you'll recognize truth when you see it.

And through this journey of half a lifetime, I've tried to remember that death—like my "foreordained" car accident—is unavoidable. That being the case, it makes no sense to live timidly.

"Life is unfair."

John F. Kennedy
Press Conference, March 1962

Patrick Dwyer

The Young Barbarians

I would have helped slash the tires, but I didn't have a knife. Later on this fact would render me technically innocent. I never told the cops that it had been my idea. In the harsh light of the police station it didn't seem important, and no one asked. My accomplices were not whiners and suffered judgement in silence.

It was the summer of 1962. John F. Kennedy, who my friends and I worshipped, was president. The 1960s were not yet *the sixties*. My heroes were still credible. All my friends were still alive. We lived in a mining town in northeastern Minnesota that was chock-full of kids. The post-World War II yen for home and family had found fertile ground. And though it was a small community, the various neighborhoods produced their own cliques and gangs that roamed the nearby woods like tribal bands.

On that day in June five from our "tribe"—Billy was twelve, John was eleven, his brothers Joe and Tim were nine and seven, and I was eleven—launched a foray into a stand of pines just west of town. At our ages, before high school more or less unified the neighborhoods (our town of 7,000 supported three large grade schools in those fecund days), our loyalties were narrow. The area encompassed by

7

four or five city blocks was home. The next town, the state, the nation, were abstractions. Our gang of two dozen or so kids was preeminent.

When we encountered other groups, it was with cautious tolerance or, often, open hostility. This was a short-lived, harmless kind of prejudice. It was fun, and the rivalry was perhaps necessary, a means to aid the development of a personal identity in the midst of a practically homogenous population. We think of big cities as being regimented, like teeming human anthills, where faceless people rush about at the mercy of mass transit and, perhaps, "Big Brother." But life for life, a small town, inherently maternalistic, can exert far more pressure to conform than the indifferent metropolis. The big city may channel a person's movements into the same streets and tunnels that confine millions of others, but it cares not what that person believes. A small town allows a lad to wander where he will, in alley, street, or field, but his mind is closely monitored.

And we did roam, children high on the parole of summer, accentuating differences that didn't exist. That day, we patrolled the pines and played "war." We weren't yet enthralled with Vietnam (nor was the Pentagon), and nobody said much about Korea. World War II was not yet history, the subject of anniversary retrospectives on the evening news; it was what our fathers had done just before we were born. Like them, in our play we fought the Japs and the Nazis, and, if our governments were now friendly, we at least had not forgotten Pearl Harbor. We gazed in awe at the .25-caliber Arisaka rifle (and bayonet) that Billy's father had brought home from the Pacific Theater and hung in his garage. War was just. Battle was a game. We simply couldn't imagine otherwise.

However, imagination is what got us into trouble. While playing, we stumbled across three bicycles lying in the woods. They weren't brand new, but they weren't junkers either. A cursory look would have shown that they had been resting there a short time, and that someone cared for them. But I imagined aloud that the perfectly serviceable bikes had been abandoned, that someone—for reasons I couldn't specify—had left them in the woods instead of taking them to the dump. They belonged to no one and were, therefore, fair game. I suggested we wreck them.

Most of the boys I knew possessed a streak of barbarism; acts of petty vandalism were frequent. It was a delight to dismember a snowman, flatten a sand castle, or heave a rock through a garage window (house windows were generally sacrosanct). We even destroyed our own things. I remember taking a model airplane I had built and blowing it up with a firecracker. A friend used charcoal lighter to set one of his model ships aflame. It seems twisted and demented, but most of us were like that, and we weren't abnormal. We were kids— ignorant and immature, behaving more like the dogs we ran with than little human beings.

So I didn't have to coax my buddies into vandalizing the bicycles. It was a familiar pleasure, this pointless destruction. John and his two brothers had just received small pocket knives from their father, impressive status symbols much prized by us all. Billy and I were unarmed, but I proposed that the brothers slash the tires of the bikes, hoping they'd let us borrow their knives to make a few slices ourselves. They wouldn't oblige, hogging all the cutting for themselves, but that was their privilege, and Billy and I didn't force the issue.

We could have done a lot more damage to the bikes, but when the tires were flat and rent asunder, we were spooked by sounds in the woods and ran. With the deed done, my theory about the bikes was no longer convincing, and we were afraid it was a big mistake. Even so, we didn't see any way we could be caught. We certainly didn't imagine another kid could be so corrupt and nefarious as to squeal on us. Nevertheless, we were betrayed.

On our way into the woods we had met Phil, a casual acquaintance from another part of town. He was busy attempting to ignite grass fires, and we had spoken with him briefly before moving on to our own misdeeds. Later, when the angry parents of the young girls who owned the bikes confronted him, Phil turned them onto us. Within a few hours of the crime he led them to John's house, where we were all holed up in the garage. We were shocked and scandalized. For long afterwards, whenever any of us encountered Phil we pelted him with rocks. (Several years later, when he was fired from a job, it happened that I was the one who took his place. The childish animosity was long gone, but the irony of it all was still satisfying.)

I don't know who called the cops, but, I suspect, it was John's father. No doubt he made restitution for the tires and saw an opportunity to teach us something. He ordered us to wait on his porch for the police and give ourselves up. We were terrified but feeling honorable. Our guilt was being expiated; it was not an entirely unpleasant sensation.

But the police capitalized on the fearfulness of the situation. They played their role flawlessly. The squad car pulled into the street with its beacon flashing, attracting the attention of curious neighbors. As the five of us squeezed into the back seat, we heard the doors lock as they closed, and the policemen frowned at us through a metal screen between the seats. They briefly discussed slapping us into handcuffs and only reluctantly decided against it. Feeling tiny and helpless, we sank as far back into the seat as we could.

Though we would brag about our experience later, relishing a fleeting notoriety, we didn't feel heroic inside the car. It was an event that indelibly branded my mind. I was a prisoner, a defenseless captive of big men with guns. They informed us that we were "under arrest," and, though the cops were probably striving mightily to keep straight faces, I was utterly intimidated by the reality of *force*. Later, as my academic education proceeded, I would learn about cultural and sociological phenomena that help bind societies together, but in that squad car I experienced one of the basic motivations of social cohesion: Fear. The fear of force and the force of fear, outlaw against society and society against outlaw in a battle fired by dread.

At the police station our lesson continued in earnest. The officers guided us on a tour of the jail cells, and their stark, barren cleanliness was disturbing. They looked like hospital rooms. We were shown a padded cell and told that it was where boys like us belonged. But that didn't make sense because the room resembled a carnival funhouse. However, any thoughts of levity were quickly extinguished when the police chief himself, looking more menacing in suit and tie than his officers did in uniform, delivered a stern dressing down. He interrogated us one by one, demanding to know if we'd slashed the tires. Billy and I answered no. We were too scared for more than monosyllabic replies. John, Joe, and Tim confessed, and the chief wrote their names in a book and informed them they now had a *record*. It was one of the most ominous things I've ever heard. The chief was just winding down his lecture when a terrible thing happened.

Billy's father, flushed with rage, barged into the police station. His wife had summoned him home from the mine, telling him that his boy was in police custody. The man shouted at the cops, bitterly furious that they'd dared pick up his son. I thought for a moment he was going to hit someone. Until then the five of us had been stoically, if fearfully, standing up and taking our punishment. There was a certain pride in it. But now Billy, who hadn't touched a tire nor come up with the idea but who, nevertheless, had stuck with the rest of us, was humiliated. His father's wrathful tantrum on his behalf was a crushing loss of face. The rest of us lowered our heads in embarrassment as Billy, the oldest among us, burst into mortified tears. His father hustled him out of the station.

We didn't know then, of course, that Billy's young life was already almost half over. Not many years later, when I read of his violent death far from home, the painful incident in the police station was the first thing I recalled. But time had softened the recollection, mellowing the trauma into a sentimental fondness for the ill-considered, but good intentions of a father.

The police chief quickly wound up our rehabilitation session, and the brothers and I trooped out of the station into vivid sunlight, eternally grateful that our parents had stayed away.

Aside from showing up to pay parking tickets or bail friends out of jail (the crowd I run with has never been completely rehabilitated), I've managed to avoid police stations and padded cells ever since. I probably wouldn't have become a criminal anyway, but that swift and accurate blow in behalf of justice left me with a crisp impression that crime did not pay. It sounds hokey, but I survived the balance of my adolescence without so much as tipping a garbage can on Halloween. Perhaps there is such a thing as deterrence.

In any case, despite the "arrest," the entire incident was an exercise in innocence. We left the station properly chastised, cleansed of guilt. We were pure. Society, at least in that small mining town in June 1962, was confident and in control. It knew how to mete out routine justice. It believed in its standards and their clarity. There was a sense of identity. Fathers could make arrangements with the police—benevolent conspiracies against the innate wildness of boys. But that society seemed young. Despite the Depression and World War II, it was still fresh and self-righteous, at the peak of its power and insulated from many of the unattractive realities of the world. Like boys, it would grow and change, and not all the changes would be welcome.

I remember 1962 as a good year, but we couldn't remain there. It may be only illusion, fostered by nostalgia, but if we're now more calloused, more cynical, it was unavoidable. In looking back there's always a compelling sense of fate. Kennedy *had* to go to Dallas. American troops *had* to go to Vietnam. Unrest *had* to shake America. Billy *had* to die. There is little comfort in history, in remembering. What rewards exist are bittersweet.

If I'd only had a knife!

"Iron sharpens iron . . ."

Proverbs 27:17

Mark Coyle

Open Pit Playground

That small mining town was Chisholm. In the self-assured era before the American steel industry hit the skids, the town had two-hundred members in each high school graduating class and a mildly prosperous downtown. In 1908 a runaway forest fire burned it to the ground (with its four dozen saloons), and in the mid-1950s when I started school, the collective memory of the disaster was still kept fresh. We learned about it in class, along with the other trials and struggles of our immigrant grandparents and, in some cases, parents.

We were shown stark black-and-white and sepia photographs of hard-bitten people. They had come from Eastern Europe, Italy, Scandinavia, journeyed thousands of alien miles to dig for iron ore in a wild new land. I was struck by how grim they all appeared. No one ever smiled in those photos. Maybe it was a formal, Old World camera pose. Or maybe they hadn't been told the truth about northern Minnesota winters.

Poor people from the "old country" filled the mines of the Mesabi Iron Range. "Da Raynch," as the new English speakers called it, developed into a long chain of open pit and underground mines carved into the hematite, taconite, and greenstone of the Canadian

Shield. The iron that made the steel that "won two world wars" was shipped to the eastern mills from the Mesabi—meaning "Red Giant" in Ojibway. The Indians realized this land was special, knew about the iron ore, the red giant hiding underground. In the 1880s, white prospectors searching for gold stumbled upon those true riches of the region, and in a few decades men and machines created their own geography, a saw-toothed landscape of deep, ledged canyons, and dumps and stockpiles rising like hills. The interlocking string of mines, as convoluted as the surface of the moon, sprawled over 150 square miles.

Chisholm lies near the middle of the Mesabi Range, hemmed in on three sides by open pit mines. From the doorsteps to the drag-lines was never a very long walk, especially in the old days. I remember being lulled to sleep by the wail of the shift whistle in the Sherman Mine. It was soothing, like listening to loon calls by a wilderness campfire—though I imagine the grunts down in the mine didn't think that damned whistle was quite so romantic.

I was raised in that tough, flinty town, and, after a suitable span of time, commonly referred to as "growing up," I left Chisholm to seek knowledge and understanding at a college in St. Paul. I didn't remain there long enough to discover if such can be found in the Twin Cities, but one thing I did do was join an environmental action group. It was 1970, the year of Earth Day and the nativity of a widespread environmental consciousness. I was fired with the zeal of a crusader and possessed that clarity of vision, that sure awareness of right and wrong characteristic of zealots. I had no doubt what pollution was, and the battle lines were drawn in black and white.

There were reams of new literature available on the subject of ecological damage, and one of the booklets I found was a depressing little survey entitled "Our Polluted Planet." It was profusely illustrated with photos of environmental nightmares: oil spills, smog-enshrouded cities, putrid rivers. These were typical examples, and I leafed through the booklet quickly until I came to a particular photo. It purported to display a raped, ravaged landscape, and I recognized it immediately. It was the Hull Rust Mine in Hibbing, only a few miles from my hometown. I was shocked. The mines were pollution? Why, I thought, they were beautiful—red and maroon mountains and gorges that had been playgrounds for my friends and me, vast arenas for childhood games and fantasies. Yet the pamphleteers considered them disaster areas. How could that be?

For a child on the Mesabi Range the mines found an integral part of the topography, as natural as lakes and trees. I was told by parents and teachers (somewhat proudly) that the mammoth dumps and awesome pits were man-made, but it was difficult to grasp. A chasm three or four miles long and four-hundred feet deep appeared an act of God. Could our fathers and grandfathers truly have done such marvelous works? And they *were* marvelous to Range kids. Abandoned mines were playgrounds of wild immensity—our own badlands—at once familiar and exotic. We scaled cliffs, using old steel shovel cable instead of rope. We crawled into caves after uprooting the "caution" signs meant to scare us off, carelessly tossing them away like frisbees. We flung ourselves off precipices into deep green pools as cold as January. It was a miracle, I believe, that no one I knew of was ever killed. Today, at six-foot-three, two-hundred-ten pounds, I shudder to think of what I dared when I was scrawny and twelve. If our mothers had only known!

But they probably did. They knew the stain of iron ore on denim (oh, how they knew), and they also knew they couldn't stop us. After all, United States Steel couldn't. The old mines were fenced, but to us this was mere formality. The techniques for going over, under, or through barbed wire became ingrained childhood skills, like holding a baseball bat or riding a bicycle. There were mining company cops on patrol, but they never tried very hard to nab us. Perhaps they remembered how much fun it all could be, and realized anyway how futile it was to chase nimble kids who knew the pit and its dumps like a fox knows the forest.

Summers were best. At the bottom of the particular open pit mine that my buddies and I claimed as our own (just southeast of Chisholm, below where Ironworld, a mining museum/park/amphitheater now stands) was a large pool of spring water surrounded by cliffs. We suffered no shortage of conventional lakes and beaches in the area (Minnesota is, after all, "The Land of 10,000 Lakes"), but it seemed so much more delicious to swim in the pit. I suppose it was the inherent danger. The pool was icy-cold and incredibly deep. Once we hauled in one-hundred feet of rope, lashed a rock to the end, and tried to "sound" the depth. We never found out—one-hundred feet of rope wasn't enough. We were briefly entranced by the notion that the pool was bottomless, that it joined a secret underground river that flowed to the center of the earth. Why not? In those halcyon days, it seemed credible.

To enter our favorite pool, we had to leap from a fifteen-foot-high rock ledge. It would have been no big deal except that the base of the ledge sloped outward. We had to approach at a dead run and throw ourselves out as far as we could to avoid hitting jagged rocks. I remember when we first discovered the pool and studied that ledge. Even to youths convinced of their immortality, it looked risky. I was terrified at the prospect of making that all-or-nothing leap, and I'm sure the others were too. But it seems at least one in every group is willing to try anything. Our trailblazer was a husky, fearless kid named John. He was always the first one up a cable, into a cave, or off a cliff.

If he made it (and he always did), then the rest of us deemed it appropriate to follow. And you *had* to follow. All things were possible except "chickening out"—that was inconceivable. We didn't have to learn anything from the Orient about "losing face." Lose your life? Well, that was too bad, but by all means don't lose face.

The rest of us stood in scared silence as John perched on the rim of the ledge and surveyed the rock below. He flashed us a jaunty grin (as if the whole thing was being filmed) and took four or five paces backward. Then, with his usual whoop and holler, he dashed for the edge and cast himself out into sunlight and air. He cleared the base of the ledge by about a foot. We all agreed that was cutting it close. He surfaced and laughed in triumph, but I gulped. I was next.

My stomach fluttered, and my skin grew clammy as I stood atop that ledge. Years later, as I sat in roaring prop blast about to make my first parachute jump, I recalled that day in the mine. For whatever dubious cause, my fate was—at least temporarily—in my own hands, and from some mysterious and slightly deranged region of the mind, I dredged up whatever it required to run and leap off that cliff. Sitting in the jump plane about to leap again, I fondly, if nervously, remembered that, as I sprinted off the ledge, one of those turkeys had yelled, "I get your stamp collection!" The wrong joke at the right time can be comforting. My buddies told me I cleared the base of the ledge by about *two* feet.

I guess it was yet another improvised rite of passage. Anyway, that's more palatable than thinking it was merely stupid. But our play wasn't all reckless derring-do. We spent hours drawing detailed maps of "our" mine and thinking up esoteric names for the features of our private universe. In one spot, the excavations formed a high, wooded plateau. We dubbed this "The Lost World," harkening to a sci-fi film about twentieth century dinosaurs discovered on an isolated mesa. It was our citadel and sanctuary. We had a campsite, lookout posts, and cache. No matter what childhood (and adolescent) trials and anxieties assailed us, we always had a place to go. We never told any adults about it. Such information was too sensitive for grown-up ears. Parents, teachers, policemen—none could follow us there. Fears, worries, and doubts could be left behind. In a location so well-loved and so well-defended, even dreams could survive.

It's ironic. In a place that would later serve as yet another example of "Our Polluted Planet," we nurtured our interest in nature. We hunted for (and found) fossils. We marveled at birches growing out of clefts in bedrock. We observed woodchucks, foxes, and crayfish. We examined geologic strata bared before us like an open book. From the tops of man-made mountains, we surveyed the form of the earth—from horizon to horizon we saw the land on a grand scale, a scale that suggested possibilities. These were our high places, and from them we learned the constellations.

There was a time, before the "natural," or high-grade ore was depleted, when most Range homes had a reddish-colored rug on the back porch. When our fathers came home from the mine, they wiped their boots and shed their red overalls on that rug. The various rugs may have started out black or brown or gray, but all ended up looking the same. The streets were full of dusty red cars, and when they were washed the gutters ran red. For years I associated being dirty with being red (with no political connotations), for it was the same with us kids. Instead of green grass stains and black mud, our jeans were permeated with red dust. Where our fathers toiled, we romped, and our mothers got upset. They tacitly forbid us to be miners when we grew up, and there we were already, as encrusted with iron ore as the old man was after day shift.

But our mothers needn't have worried. The abandoned mines didn't give us a taste for mining—they offered a taste for adventure, for exploration and discovery. They gave us a yen for scaling heights and an appreciation for freedom. We wandered where we would, and U.S. Steel's fences meant nothing.

Scars upon the face of the planet? Yes, technically speaking, I suppose so. But fortunately, unlike the strip mines of the eastern coal fields, the iron mines were confined to a narrow geographical band, and local vegetation is making a comeback. There's mineland reclamation going on—removal of old structures, tree-planting and fertilization, the stocking of pools with trout. Who could oppose that? But there's also been some idle talk of leveling the dumps and filling the pits. It would be astronomically—no doubt, prohibitively—expensive, and what purpose would it serve? Do you raze playgrounds? Do you bury swimming holes? Do you re-conceal fossils and alter the landscape of memories? No. Not if you're concerned with a healthy environment. And that, at least partly, is a place where happy bands of kids can play and grow and be free. We did and we were. And we'll never be quite so free again.

"Verily, I have often laughed at the weaklings who thought themselves good because they had no claws."

Nietzsche

Fred Yiran

Out for Blood

By age fifteen things got serious. Before that our violence had been confined to "playing war" and an occasional fight with a playmate. But when we signed up for high school football, the violence became focused and organized. As young American males, we were being bred for war. (Our biology teacher mentioned his World War II exploits on Saipan and assured the boys in the class that we would soon have our "chance for service"—in Vietnam.) Even as sophomores on the "B" team, it was important to separate the "men" from the boys.

Our coach relied on suffering. An otherwise cheery French instructor, he was a ruthless taskmaster on the field. During the last two sweltering weeks in August, he drilled us into the ground—two and one-half hours in the morning and the same in the afternoon. The shriek of his whistle haunted my sleep. Forty-three kids went out for the team, and by the first game only twenty-six remained. We had a taste of boot camp.

It was a brutalization process. By means of deliberate and time-honored practice techniques, we were acclimated to the delivery and acceptance of pain. Our goal was to become as intimidating as pos-

19

sible. Once, the coach told me I wasn't "mean enough" to play defense. But that aptitude can be acquired; the more one gets hit, the easier it becomes to hit back. One of the kindest things a coach could say was: "He likes to hit."

And we did. After two or three seasons of football it was like a mild narcotic. Before a game the tension and fear were almost painful. Stomachs fluttered, palms sweat, and nervous fingers adjusted and readjusted helmets and pads that were already perfectly in place. To help relieve this condition we would vigorously pound on each other, bashing shoulders or butting heads like dueling bighorn sheep.

But our adversaries were artificial. The other team, trying hard to hate us from across the field, had no claim on our lives or property. We were determined to punish, hurt, and defeat them, not for the sake of survival or territorial imperatives, but for the appeasement of manufactured egos. We'd seen the fans on TV chanting, "Kill, Bubba, Kill!" It seemed glorious, glamorous.

Immediately before kickoffs, excitement reached a noisy peak as our fans shouted for touchdowns, tackles, and blood. Their vicarious enjoyment of the battle goaded us on. The cheers, yells, and boos carried out over the field, providing a curious counterpoint to the crunch of pads and cries of pain. We avidly sought their approval.

At the tender age of sixteen, one of my teammates was already affectionately known as "Mad Dog." He was mean enough to play defense. From his position at right tackle he reveled in personal combat. He was a big boy, strong and heavy, and he usually gained the upper hand. I recall one game when he was performing even better than usual. His opponent, a smaller, much weaker kid, was beaten and helpless to the point of desperation. Mad Dog was steadily hammering him into a state of total ineffectiveness. Both the physical and psychological struggles seemed to be about over when the hapless kid had a stroke of inspiration. On a third-down pass play, when he knew Mad Dog would try to charge by him and flatten the quarterback, he didn't resist. At the snap of the ball he simply laid down. True to form, Mad Dog wildly barged in. He tripped over the prostrate blocker and fell flat on his face. As the defensive team left the field, and we of the offense trotted on, I laughed and kidded him about his humiliation. Mad Dog wasn't smiling. He glared at me and growled, "If he does that again, I'm going to stomp on his back!"

Several minutes later, with our defense in again, there was a commotion on the field and the game was whistled to a halt. A stretcher was hurried out and Mad Dog's opponent carried off. The lad's stratagem hadn't worked twice. I looked down at my spiked shoes and cringed. Mad Dog was grinning. Unlike a canine, he'd been trained to be rabid; his fangs were on his feet.

I understood the satisfaction of violence. I played on the offensive line and was usually pitted "man" against "man," dueling with the defensive lineman—blocking, hitting, grabbing, shoving, fighting. In one particularly bitter contest, I became thoroughly enmeshed in a struggle for domination. Time after time I collided with my opponent, striving to cast him aside. He fought back, lunging and pummeling, but late in the game I sensed victory.

Before each play our opposing lines hunkered down into crouched stances, and in this position, through the limited field of view within my helmet, all I could see were my opponent's legs. There, on his right shin, was a trickle of blood. It flowed from beneath his knee pad, twisted through the hair on his battered skin, and disappeared into his sock. I was fascinated, jubilant. I had probably caused this wound. I had drawn the blood everyone was screaming for. Like a hungry shark, the presence of blood drove me on. I plumbed new reserves of energy and fierceness. I wanted to see more blood, to take advantage of his pain and drive him into the ground once and for all. The game ended before I could break him. It mattered little that we lost.

Yet I was not by nature a violent kid. My last real fight had been in the seventh grade, with only a few before that. The anger and aggression I could generate on the football field was a revelation. As Kahlil Gibran wrote: "Among the people there are thieves who have not yet stolen, murderers who have not yet killed, and liars who so far have always told the truth." My potential had been awakened. I was a little afraid of what I'd seen.

Over twenty years have passed, and I haven't become a murderer. My last fight is still the one in the seventh grade. I didn't even end up in a real boot camp. But I watch football on TV; I cheer and yell and scream things like, "Nail him! Kill him!" My wife shakes her head in bewilderment—and pity. Sometimes I laugh at myself, but not very often.

I'm reminded of a scene from the movie *Patton*. George C. Scott, hard-faced and intense in the title role, approaches a battlefield. Amid burning vehicles and smoking shell holes are scattered hundreds of corpses, both German and American. The battle had been bitter, the final combat hand-to-hand. Scott surveys the carnage for a long moment and then turns to his aide: "I love it!" he says breathlessly. "God help me, but I love it so!"

And thus is my ambivalence about football, about violence. For, after that game when I'd made my opponent bleed, I faced him and we smiled. We warmly embraced, patting each other on the back, saying, "Good game, good game."

"The first requisite of a good citizen
in this Republic of ours is that
he shall be able and willing to pull his weight."

Theodore Roosevelt

Mark Coyle

The 8-Sweep

It's probably an illusion, a view distorted by the plain passage of time, but the problems and priorities of twenty-five years ago seem uncomplicated. No doubt these matters are relative; I suspect point of view is everything—not to mention hindsight. If I could be transported back into a teen-aged state of mind, I'd probably discover that anxieties are anxieties, and stress has the same effect whether caused by the spectre of nuclear winter or the agony of acne. In 1966 it was: To make that block.

To make that damned block. It mattered more than anything else in all the orange autumn world. Concentration was the key. You must forbid yourself to be distracted by extraneous action—the crunch of pads, the grunts of contact, the divots thrown up by digging spikes. You must not "telegraph" your coming move, unconsciously orienting your body stance in the direction of the play. A savvy linebacker would pick up on that and make you eat dirt.

The play was called the 8-Sweep. The quarterback took the snap, faked a hand-off to the fullback, and pitched out to a halfback who was already sprinting toward the right end of the line. We liked to run the sweep when we'd been pummeling a team up the middle, having our way with them at the center of the line. They would be "softened up," a little battered, but still aware that the straight-ahead drive could be setting them up for something else. They expected a ruse, but the logical maneuver would be a draw play—send the fullback barging up the middle like all he saw was daylight and headlines, but don't hand him the ball. Let him cradle empty folded arms, his helmet down and knees pounding. Let him perform. The linebackers at least had to look at him. And if the snap was smooth and the quarterback quick, he could then fire a hot one to a receiver cruising out in the flat. That's what the defense was looking for.

So when we knew they were nervous about the middle, worried about lost yards and waiting for the draw and an aerial assault, we hit them with the 8-Sweep. It could be devastating. But only if I made that block.

I played right guard on the offensive line, and the integral cog in the works of the 8-Sweep was my "pulling" from the line. On paper it was simple. At the snap of the ball, I'd pivot to the right and start running along behind the line of scrimmage. Theoretically, the center would hit the defensive tackle I was normally tangling with—cutting him down from the side as he greedily charged into the unexpected hole I'd left behind. In three seconds the play would be "developed." I would be turning downfield just beyond the end of the line. Our left guard would also have pulled (his normal opponent was to be taken out by the faking fullback), and be right behind me. We'd serve as a phalanx for the halfback who'd be trailing us both. The defense, that is, those who were still standing, would see what was going down and one or two linebackers and a couple of defensive backs would be surging toward the right side of the field. Being the spearhead of our offensive, I had to make that first block. If I missed it, the play would self-destruct, crumpling into chaos and leaving the halfback to scramble and claw for whatever yards he could gain (or lose) on his own.

Pull out, run, block. Simple. You could probably train a dog to do it. But there were twenty-one people out there, each doing his own little grass-stained minuet, and nearly any one of them, friend or foe, could ruin the operation. If the center missed his block, the opposing tackle would be in the backfield almost as soon as the ball. We're talking disaster—like dropping a loose bolt into a transmission. He could throw the halfback for a loss, cripple the quarterback, or, if you hadn't been living right, he could even intercept the pitchout. If our right tackle was pushed back by the defense, I could bump into him and never make it to the end of the line. If our backs muffed the ball-handling, I'd get there too soon. If their backs read the play instantly and blitzed, I'd get there too late. A hundred things could go wrong. (And of course I could always trip, slip, or stumble sans the assistance of anyone else.)

And so Coach Doyle drilled us in the execution of that sweep. He liked it. He liked the fluid precision, the pulling guards, the fake, the grace of the pitchout. He liked to devastate the other guys. But above all, it seemed to me, he liked a good block.

That's what he expected of me: a slick, potent, play-making block. But he was working against himself. As a high school coach he was determined to teach more than football. He wanted to instill character and champion good old Puritan virtues. He appeared to see the playing field as a microcosm of the planet, the game as a template for Life. He wanted to reward hard work. The starting positions on his team went not necessarily to the flashiest, most gifted athletes, but to those who were the most diligent in practice. He made it clear at the start of the season: whoever *worked* would play.

And so he was stuck with me. I was slow, clumsy, and even a bit timid. I wasn't a natural athlete. But man, did I work. I attacked the wind sprints at full bore, always hustling, drilling like a berserker. I radiated sincerity and honest effort. If he was going to keep his word, he couldn't avoid installing me as a starter, a member of the exalted first string.

At the end of practice the day before each weekly game, he'd announce the starters. To hear my name read off that clipboard was a confirmation of basic worth. It was a consecration. As an insecure teen-aged male, raised in a man's world and expected to be strong, brave, and physically competent, I knew what mattered to my peers—what mattered, apparently, to the world. When my name echoed through that militant, macho locker room, I was a man among men. I had arrived.

But I was still a clutz, and I had trouble with the 8-Sweep. First there was that humiliation during practice. While we were scrimmaging one day the coach kept inserting the sweep into the day's repertoire, and every time we tried it the defense killed us. Finally one of the linebackers admitted that he knew when the sweep was going to be run because I was telegraphing the play. He could tell by my stance at the line when I was preparing to pull out for the downfield block. The coach scowled, and I was close to embarrassed tears.

And there was the mechanics of the play. Being a high school team, we didn't always operate like a well-oiled machine. Tactics often got a little snarled and confused without the play actually coming completely apart. That's where agility and quickness came in. A good athlete could take miscues in stride and still make the plan work. But if I was thrown off—bumped by the right tackle or nearly tripped up by a lunging defensive end—it was usually all over. I was too slow and ungainly to effectively recover.

And then there was fear. I had no difficulty with violent contact at close quarters. In the "pit" at the line of scrimmage, where most of my activity for an entire game encompassed two or three yards of territory, I could hit and be hit without qualms. But when I was upright and running, aiming to make contact at high speed, I turned a little chicken. Downfield blocking scared me, and sometimes when I missed the 8-Sweep block, I wasn't sure whether it was ineptness or fear of being hurt. It troubled me. Was I a coward? Was I a liability on the 8-Sweep?

But the coach persevered. He was caught in the benevolent net of his own convictions and promises. I worked, therefore I played. He couldn't bench me, and I liked to think he didn't want to. Instead, he encouraged, cajoled, and critiqued. He hunkered down on the line himself and we went through the motions step by step. The stance—three-pointed and stable, straight ahead and level. The pivot—raise to a crouch, turn the right foot parallel to the line and follow with the rest of the body. Run—even steps and balanced, head up and watching the flow of the play. The cut—sharply downfield and into the traffic, aligned with the halfback, not too close, nor too far ahead. The block—hit low and hard, shoulder first, use your momentum and weight. Over and over, dry runs and scrimmages.

I fantasized about the sweep and the block. I featured myself in heroic scenarios; the 8-Sweep as blitzkrieg, a cavalry charge for touchdowns and glory. I watched the sweep on TV, executed in its quintessential form by the Green Bay Packers. Jerry Kramer at right guard and Fuzzy Thurston at left, smoothly pulling out and churning downfield like Sherman tanks, a moving wall for Paul Hornung; another first down.

That autumn it was the best thing I could conceive. To pull out and make that block—perfectly. It represented manhood, acceptance. It was a gritty, unforgiving test of will. I wanted to please the coach. I lusted for approbation and respect.

And one day I got it—during a practice scrimmage. It was full contact, the real thing. All we lacked were fans and our dress uniforms. (But it was late in the season and both were expendable anyway.) The quarterback called the 8-Sweep, and I immediately tensed. Concentrate. We trotted up to the line, and I eased into my lineman's stance—straight, level, normal. Keep it nondescript. On the count of two the center delivered a clean snap, and even as I pivoted I could see he was going to make his block stick.

For the moment I was free, running behind the mass of collisions. The halfback was just collecting the pitchout and was running ahead of me, parallel, but five yards further behind the line. Good. On the other side, a linebacker and the safety had now read the play and were scooting to the right. Their eyes were fixed on the halfback. As I reached the point where I should cut downfield, I realized neither of them was seeing me. I was still free—an undetected missile, a forgotten trump card. Our left guard was right behind me. He and I and the halfback made our practiced, synchronized cut. The two defenders slashed in. My sights were on the linebacker. He was hungry for the tackle. We closed rapidly. Impact.

The timing of the hit was automatic. Drill and eagerness had, for the moment, overcome fear. I launched my left shoulder in a driving, diving roll. I hit him just above the ankles, angling in front from his right side. He never saw me. Nothing hurt. The block felt smooth and light, like a front roll on a thick mat. The linebacker hit the ground on his shoulder and back and laid there. We ended up side by side, looking at each other. His face was blank with incomprehension. He stared at me as if I'd fallen from the sky. He was stunned, not by pain, but by total surprise. Finally he said, "Beautiful block, man."

Downfield the left guard was pushing the safety aside, and the halfback was scampering for the end zone. The coach blew his whistle and spit it out. He strode over to where I was rising off the ground. He wasn't smiling; this was a solemn event. It was beyond a mere grin, and he knew it.

"That," he said, with almost formal inflection, "is the best block you ever made."

I swelled up, turned red, and mumbled a "thank you." The linebacker slapped my helmet. It was one of the happiest moments of my young life. To make that block. Simple.

But the years passed. The 8-Sweep was not life, and the field was not a microcosm of the planet. Pity. Because for one green moment I understood it all.

"For modes of faith let graceless zealots fight . . ."
Alexander Pope

Patrick Dwyer

Quarterback Keeper

I didn't like Rob. He was cocky and smart-mouthed for no good reason. A lot of guys were arrogant, but at least with cause—they were strong or fast or tough, or maybe all three. A good football player could be excused a bit of swagger, especially at age fifteen.

But Rob was lousy. If he had played another position he might have done better, but he wanted to be a quarterback. Nothing required more athletic ability, football savvy, and leadership skills, and Rob was average or below in all those categories. But he needed the glory. He featured himself a signal-caller because that was the romantic, high-profile position.

So he became our third-string quarterback and spent most of his time on the bench. Nevertheless he still strutted, he still fired off the smart-ass remarks as if he had the right. His pride and haughtiness were so out of proportion to his talent that it was embarrassing. If he had taken the role of meek underdog trying to make good, he could have been accepted. But being a brash hot dog cost him dearly in simple fellowship. By posturing as a star he made himself an outsider. There were other poor players on the squad, but they didn't put on airs and were thus considered members of the team—at least

29

in the social, if not the functional sense. Rob was ridiculed—often. To fight back he got sassier, and his fortunes spiraled into a vicious circle of wounded pride and petty recrimination.

The cruelty of adolescent boys is relentless, but Rob had a stubborn streak that buoyed him through tides of abuse. I wondered at the confidence, audacity, meanness, or whatever it was that allowed him to resist reality so doggedly. I expected him to quit the team or curb his mouth, but he did neither, clinging to his desire like a taloned cat, tenacious in his faith that he was a quarterback and deserved to play.

His belief may have been fueled by the fact that we weren't the "A" team. We were the "B" squad, ninth and tenth graders being groomed for future service and glory on the varsity. We had our own official games, but they were weekday afternoon contests that were largely ignored. The stands were usually sprinkled with a few parents and girl friends, and we never had anything approaching a crowd. There were no cheerleaders, loudspeakers, or reporters. Rob probably felt that he was good enough (if not too good) for the "B" league.

But despite the lack of fanfare, or perhaps because of it, there was a certain elemental purity to "B" squad games. Our team was an isolated but coherent unit, devoted to itself. We weren't performing for a crowd, or even conspicuously representing the school; we were playing for the integrity of the team as an unheralded, independent entity. With almost no outside attention focused on us we were forced to be self-sufficient. Freed from the distractions of Friday night hoopla, we could play the game for its own sake.

In that milieu, it was easier to appreciate the values of organized sport. As mentioned, our coach was a tireless autocrat who believed that hard work should be and would be honored. Endless drills were the route to the Promised Land. He established rules, enforced them consistently, and thus built our faith in the system. He immersed us in a world of order and justice. It was a quasi-religious sphere where sincere effort and good works were rewarded, and sloth and failure were punished. Only the best people would play, only the best teams would win, and the best were the hardest workers. This simple philosophy drove me like an engine, and I readily offered sweat and blood. I was a zealot, and week after week I started.

But I also had more modest aspirations than Rob. I was right guard on the offensive line—a basic, grind-it-out, pound-it-out blocker. Sure, I had fantasies of more glorious roles, but I concentrated on being a scrimmaging grunt.

An important part of my mission was to protect the quarterback. One of the dogmas burned into linemen's brains was that our quarterback was sacrosanct. To allow the opposition to touch him, much less tackle him, was a terrible sin. Rarely have I felt shame as painfully as I did on the occasions when I failed to protect my quarterback during a "B" squad football game. We were programmed for competition, aggression, and victory. We had thorough training (not all of it valuable), but, strangely enough, third-string Rob, the irritating loudmouth, afforded me one of the most vivid lessons.

It was our second game of the season, and, toward the end of the fourth quarter, victory seemed assured. The score was 13 to 0, but that didn't reflect how completely we had dominated the field. Our second-string quarterback had played most of the final period, and, with only a few minutes left, the coach felt confident enough to send Rob off the bench to finish it.

We had a third down with five yards to go at the fifty-yard line. The normal call would have been an off-tackle running play, or perhaps a pass—though even our starting quarterback threw sparingly. In any case, it was not a critical situation. If we had to punt, the enemy would be deep in their own territory and they hadn't generated much offense all day.

But Rob sprang off the bench and sprinted out to the huddle with fire in his eye. Here was a shot at glory. His excitement was barely in check, and I expected him to call a pass play. But Rob crouched on one knee and said: "Quarterback-keeper, up the middle, on one." Of course. Even a flashy completed pass meant Rob would have to share the glory with the receiver. He wanted sole ownership of the ball and the yardage. (Blockers were always indispensable, and for that very reason we didn't figure into the glory equation.)

It was a dumb call. A quarterback-keeper was a short-yardage play that we rarely used. It put the quarterback at risk, and I hated it. If we were a yard or a half-yard shy of a critical first down (or the goal line), we might try to punch the quarterback through, but with five yards to go in a sewn-up game, it was pure self-indulgence. There were snickers in the huddle. Nevertheless, we clapped our hands, broke, and trotted up to the line of scrimmage.

It so happened that the middle linebacker of the opposing team was the cousin of a close friend, and we knew each other well—we had been bantering back and forth the whole game. As I got to the line he looked me in the eye and grinned. He said: "Quarterback-keeper, up the middle, on one."

My heart sank. I thought Rob had been rather loud in the huddle, but I didn't think it had carried across the field. The linebacker quickly spread the word among his teammates, and, as we crouched down along the line, all the players on the field knew the play and the signal, and knew that everyone else knew. Except for Rob, apparently. Even on the "B" squad he had the option of calling an audible and changing the play right then and there. Or he could've asked for a time-out. But he was charged up, oblivious to all but his own desire. The play would stand.

The linebacker was actually chuckling with anticipation, and I inwardly groaned. My head was going to be smack in the middle of the ensuing mass collision. The center, the other guard, and I were the spearhead of the play, and the entire opposing team was going to dive into our faces and smash us. But then I thought, "Good!" because they would also smash Rob. It would serve him right. I maliciously hoped they'd knock him out of the game and put him back on the sidelines where he belonged.

Rob nestled up to the center and called out, "Set! . . . Hut!" The line exploded, and in a moment I was buried in a shoving tangle of bodies. The play had collapsed instantly. Or so I thought.

With my faceguard crammed into the turf, I heard the voice of the linebacker somewhere above me: "What the hell . . .?" Then there was a cheer from our side of the field. Somehow Rob had ended up nine yards downfield. Through a bizarre quirk of luck and physics he had a first down. Only their cornerback had come between Rob and a damned touchdown. I was flabbergasted. For the first and only time I was disappointed to see a teammate do well. Only the best were supposed to succeed; only the best *deserved* to succeed. Our arrogant, self-serving quarterback should have been buried alive— punished for his sin. But there he was, grinning so hard it was almost a laugh, and sauntering back to the huddle as if he were Unitas Tarkenton Starr.

Howard Cosell once said, "Sports is the toy department of human life." He realized how seriously we consider our toys. We had just run what's called a "play," but, in spite of Rob's antics, I saw nothing playful or funny. It was a dismal moment. Certainly it wasn't the first time I'd witnessed injustice—far from it. But all the drilling, training, and locker room philosophy had seduced me into a state of false contentment. It was akin to fanatical religion or rabid politics, and Rob had exposed me to a potent heresy. It was now obvious—the precious dogma of "the best" was flawed. But I'd known that, of course. Rob had merely stripped away my own wishful faith. I'd been a zealot because, like many true believers, I needed zeal to squelch my doubts. It's a dangerous way to live, to play. And in a couple years I was to see how hazardous life can be.

"Political power grows out of the barrel of a gun."

Mao Tse-tung

Fred Yiran

A .44 Magnum Manifesto

My job was to open beer bottles and load guns. I hadn't volunteered for it, and like any draftee I was intimidated. I did as I was told, hoping for survival, and soon the backseat and floor of the old Ford were littered with bent bottle caps and spent shell casings.

There I was, Mr. "A" student, a quiet, cleancut virgin—seventeen years old and never been drunk, stoned, or even kept after school. I was a stalwart in catechism class, and the year before I'd attended early-morning Mass all forty days of Lent. Since that fear-of-God brush with the law at age eleven, I hadn't so much as tipped over a garbage can on Halloween. But now, on a moonless night in northern Minnesota, I was helpless, gripped by fear—a dread of getting caught, a terror of being killed.

Of my four companions, I had just met three that evening. It was a "friends of a friend" situation, and my buddy Jeff—also seventeen—was squeezed next to me in the backseat, swilling beer and looking cool. This excursion had been billed as "going for a little cruise," and once in the car there was nothing to do but praise the Lord and pass the ammunition. Though we were shattering a range of laws from vandalism and trespassing to most traffic regulations,

I quickly discovered our chief mission was the shining and shooting of deer.

It'd been drilled into my conscience that this was heinous—not only a gross violation of cultural standards, but also a crime against Nature. Only armed robbery or homicide was worse.

My new acquaintances—all in their twenties—clearly relished the initiation of teenagers into this dangerous game. I looked like the nerd I was, my fear apparent. Nothing enhances the flavor of outlawry like having a captive, cowed audience. In that sense, I was a hostage.

Ed was the kingpin. He was big, ugly, and a natural bully. The other two had obviously been under his sway for years—probably their whole lives. He seemed perpetually tense, as if always about to throw a punch. His congenital rage was amplified by alcohol, and he barked commands and hurled curses from the passenger seat, brandishing one of his two pistols. He had a .22 automatic and a .44 magnum revolver with a long black barrel. He shot every road sign we passed, grasping the huge .44 with both meaty hands. The signs, wobbling on their posts, clanged like bells, and Ed hooted. When a gun was empty, he'd shove it back at me or Jeff, and we'd quickly cram cartridges into the clip or cylinder. Every other time, we'd hand him a beer with his loaded gun. Empty bottles were sent flying off into the ditches, and though I also considered that a crime against Nature, I realized that being cited for littering was the least of our worries.

The Cat was driving. He wore a cowboy hat, "shit-kickers," and a constant grin. He always said "please" for another beer, and I liked him. Though he did as Ed ordered, he had a subtle control over the bully. Whenever Ed got carried away—for instance, when he missed a sign and flew into a fit, hammering the dash with a fist, a bottle, or both, the Cat would drawl, "Now Ed, watch your blood pressure." Ed would snarl, "Fuck you!" but he'd always settle down. Though piloting, the Cat insisted on cradling a semi-automatic .22 rifle in his arms, firing with one hand, steering with the other. He kept his beer bottle clutched between his thighs.

The third guy was Don—gawky, unkempt, and essentially Ed's slave. If Jeff and I hadn't been there, it would've been Don who handled the beer and bullets. Everything he said sounded stupid, and nobody paid attention to him. He was crammed into the back seat with us, hugging his Winchester .30-.30. In the confines of the car it boomed like a cannon, and I flinched each time he fired.

The tactics were simple. We'd careen down the main county highway, or twist down nameless dirt backroads, guns blazing—at signs, rabbits, skunks, beer cans, or an occasional mailbox. Ed and Don had six-cell flashlights to pick out targets in the ditches or at the edge of the woods, but what they really sought were the wide spaces of abandoned fields.

Northern Minnesota is harsh country for agriculture. Settlers labored mightily at clearing marginal land and battling eternal winters. After one or two generations, much of the unprofitable ground was surrendered to encroaching forest. Instead of cattle, the overgrown pastures now support grazing whitetails. All three gunners had their favorite spots, and we assaulted them one by one.

The Cat would find a wide, shallow stretch of ditch, and with a piercing whoop he'd gun the engine and swerve off the road. The weather had been dry, so there was no standing water, but always a vein of mud. We'd hit the quagmire at full bore, tires spinning and black globs splattering the doors. We kept our heads low so they wouldn't slam against the roof as the Cat powered the Ford up the far side of the ditch and jolted into the field. Then we were "free," unconfined by the lanes and byways of civilization.

With headlights on high-beam, and flashlights panning the darkness, the Cat weaved through tall grass, dodging clumps of hazel brush and running over aspen saplings and young balsams. The fields were rough, and the leaf springs groaned as we bounced around the back seat. I was nervously mindful that these fields often had large rockpiles, and if the Cat steered into one of those . . .

Then Don yelled, "Eyes! Eyes!" and he and Ed opened fire. One of Don's ejected shells ricocheted off the roof and hit my cheek. It was hot. "Low eyes!" snorted Ed. "Only a damned skunk!" But he was smiling.

There were no deer in the first two fields we ravaged, and I was encouraged. Maybe we wouldn't find any, and the guys would tire and quit. But I suspected it was false hope. As we squealed back onto the asphalt Ed growled, "If we don't find deer we're gonna go find one of them filthy cows!" Oh great. "Gimme another beer!" I hopped to it. One way or another, something big was going to die.

The third field had a short driveway—culvert and all—so we didn't charge the ditch. Inspired by the luxury, the Cat floored it, and we roared across the pasture at highway speed. He was laughing with pleasure.

Immediately Ed hollered, "Eyes! Deer Eyes!" I could see them in the beam of his light—a half-dozen greenish pairs across the field to our right—like fireflies. They winked in and out of view as Ed's arm bounced with the car. Don blasted away with the Winchester. The Cat spun the wheel to the right and I gasped—there was a huge rockpile. He fought the wheel with both hands, leaning way over. I leaned with him, involuntarily trying to make the Ford turn tighter. We just missed the pile, but the left front tire struck a stray rock with such force that we all hit the roof.

"There goes my alignment!" the Cat chortled.

"I got one! I got one!" yelled Don. He'd fired three or four shots before we hit the rock, and then got bashed against the window post with the rifle jammed to his face. His nose was bleeding, but he was grinning. "I got one!"

"Bullshit!" Ed spat. No way Don could have hit a deer at that range from a speeding, lurching car—him drunk besides—unless he'd been incredibly lucky. The Cat steered us toward where we'd last seen eyes. He slowed, and we all peered ahead, searching for a carcass. I prayed there wouldn't be one.

Suddenly Ed lunged across the seat and slapped the headlight switch. "Stop the car!" he hissed. In an instant it was dark and silent. He pointed behind us. "Look."

My heart froze. There was a pair of headlights on the highway. It was just after midnight, and we hadn't seen another vehicle for hours.

"Sheriff?" Don croaked.

"Shut-up!" Ed replied.

I was weak with fear. I had an urge to kick open the door and run—dash off to hide in the woods—but I was paralyzed. I didn't think Ed would let me go. Besides, I had no idea where we were.

We watched the lights, and there was a communal sigh as they disappeared around a curve. I wasn't the only one holding my breath.

"Let's get out of here," Ed ordered.

The Cat started the Ford and we headed toward the road. I was trembling with relief, but without warning Ed swiveled in his seat and pointed the .44 magnum at my face. The muzzle was an inch from the end of my nose. He cocked the hammer. His voice was venomous. "If you ever tell anybody about this . . . I'll kill you!"

I was horrified. The bore of the gun was cavernous. Deep in that black hole was the nose of a large bullet. Ed's finger curled around the trigger, and, if the car hit a rut or pothole, that slug would blow my head apart. I stammered a promise to never ever mention anything to anyone. He held the gun for another long moment, then slowly lifted it away. Don laughed, but Ed shot him a wicked glance, and he clammed up. The message was: no fooling. In that car in the middle of the night I believed him with all my heart. And I hated his guts.

But I kept my promise for years. Though my home was a hundred miles from the haunts of Ed and company, I felt the power of his threat. I realized that the Cat, and certainly Don, must feel it all the time. I reasoned that Ed was simply a bully, that he probably wasn't serious about cold-blooded murder, but I had just enough doubt to keep my mouth shut. I never saw him again, but for a long time he had secret control over a piece of my life and mind. And all he had needed was a mean streak and a pistol.

Often it's bullies that rule us. Usually it's not as overt as a gun in the face, but one scary night Ed showed me what lurks beneath the veneer of civilization. It helps to know this; it makes me cunning. "Knowledge," said Francis Bacon, "is power."

But I'll never forget that a .44 Magnum is also power. And I hate it.

*"Upon such sacrifices, my Cordelia,
the gods themselves throw incense."*

Shakespeare

Mark Coyle

A Driver's Education

In the end, the deer-shining—though terrifying—had been slapstick, and a month later, when P.J. yelled—"No brakes!"—I thought he was kidding. After all, we were a couple of seventeen-year-olds with brand new drivers' licenses, and we enjoyed that kind of exuberant, spontaneous wit. I chuckled appreciatively as we rolled down the steep hill, aimed directly at a house. Then I saw his right foot pounding the brake pedal—as we speeded up. Oh damn.

We were on a quirky section of alleyway that dumped into the middle of a residential avenue in Chisholm. In a moment the stop sign flashed by on our right. As we shot across the street, we frantically looked both ways in a panic-stricken parody of what we recently had learned in Driver's Education. Fortunately there was little traffic at that evening hour, and I felt a surge of relief as we jumped the curb unscathed, passed over the sidewalk, and started across a tree-studded lawn.

We couldn't have been doing more than twenty-five to thirty miles per hour when we hit the grass, but we had a lot of inertia, and relief quickly dissipated. The old Chevrolet, circa 1958 or 1959, was armor-plated. That sucker was made out of *steel*, not aluminum and

41

fiberglass, and it had the presence of a small tank.

Scared, but with a tight grip on the wheel, P.J. managed to miss the house, but we ran over a small evergreen in the side yard and kept on rambling. P.J. yanked the parking brake, but it made no difference. In the stark glare of the headlights, objects appeared suddenly, bounding in front of the car. P.J. dodged another tree as we invaded the backyard, and then deftly steered between two clothesline poles. If there'd been laundry out to dry, we could've dragged it along with us, careening through in the finest tradition of the Keystone Cops.

By this time the novelty had worn off. I was certain we would lose our momentum somewhere in that yard, but the Chevy was still cruising. Another alley was coming up, and, to our horror, we saw what looked like a six- or eight-foot vertical drop from the yard to the roadway. We knew of places like that in town. One of us shouted—"Jump!"—and we flung open the doors and bailed out.

We hit the turf rolling, and I was extremely proud. It was just like the movies: the heroes execute a daring, dramatic stunt to save themselves from plunging over a cliff. Leaping from a moving vehicle appealed to my teen-aged sense of prowess and audacity. It's what James Dean would've done. I felt cool and brave for about a moment.

But to our chagrin the Chevy went over the "cliff" and kept on going. The six- to eight-foot vertical drop was in reality a three-foot grassy slope. The potent interaction of headlights, shadows, and fear had conjured up a mirage. The car lumbered across the alley and barrelled downhill into the next yard. It picked up speed as it headed directly for another house. P.J. and I jumped to our feet and sprinted after it. He was plaintively calling out—"Oh no, oh no, oh no . . ."—it was clear we would never reach the driver's door in time.

The Chevy missed the garage by inches, skirted a flower bed, then rammed the back porch of the house. It bounced up four concrete steps as the rear bumper ground into the sidewalk, and that finally sapped its deadly momentum. The front bumper just kissed a gas meter, slid back a few inches, then stopped—hung up on the stairs. A puddle of brake fluid formed on the top step and began to dribble over the edge onto the steps below.

Lights came on in the house as we ran up to our bleeding hulk. A man appeared at the door, his eyes wide with shock and wonder. He cracked open the door and asked if we were okay. We told him the sad story. His wife (who happened to be one of our English teachers) called the police, and in a few minutes a squad car was on the scene. The sergeant sized up the situation, called for a wrecker, then turned to P.J. and me. He was angry.

He stabbed a finger at a telephone pole back up in the first yard and demanded: "Why didn't you guys steer into that pole?"

We stared at him and nervously grinned. He was kidding, right? I was still enamored of our timely escape from the car, even though there'd been no cliff.

The sergeant wiped away our grins. "What if there'd been some kids out playing in these yards?" he snarled. "That car could've killed somebody, and you wimps jumped out! You should've hit that pole; it was your *duty*."

In a rush of shame we realized it was true. We could've steered into something "safe" immediately, even before we had reached the "cliff." We should have risked injury to ensure that no one else got hurt. It had never occured to either of us to purposely aim for a pole or a tree. The tactic certainly hadn't been mentioned in Driver's Ed.

The cop snorted and turned away, disgusted. But in thirty seconds he had taught us more civics than we had gleaned from an entire social studies textbook. I was no longer proud of our escape. True heroes would've hit that pole; real men eat dashboards. *Pro bono publico.*

"All mass movements . . . breed fanaticism, enthusiasm, fervent hope, hatred, and intolerance . . . demand blind faith and singlehearted allegiance."

Eric Hoffer

Mark Coyle

Soldier of God

I was born in 1951. That year, Edwin M. McMillan and Glenn T. Seaborg were awarded the Nobel Prize in chemistry for their discovery of plutonium. In 1959, I knelt by my bedside and prayed. I prayed that Nikita Khrushchev, then on a state visit to the United States, would remain for at least a few weeks. I reasoned that while Khrushchev was present there couldn't be nuclear war. The Soviets wouldn't attack us if their leader was here, would they? Since Khrushchev arrived I had experienced a peace of mind I hadn't known for some time. Being a member of one of the first cohorts to be born under the threat of atomic war, I had been nurtured on fear.

Until 1956, I slept with a light on in my bedroom, terrified of a bogeyman that my mother insisted did not exist. Just about the time I was finally convinced, I was old enough to grasp the meaning of "The Bomb." It definitely existed, and night lights were powerless in the struggle to keep it out of my mind.

In 1967, Red China detonated its first hydrogen bomb, American warplanes raided Hanoi, and I first listened to a man named Garner Ted Armstrong on the radio. He said I didn't need to worry about nuclear war, Vietnam, the population explosion, or environmental catastrophe. He said he knew solutions to these problems, and he stated it convincingly. Out of fear, hope, and curiosity, I sent for free literature.

By 1969, I was awaiting Parousia. Garner Ted's booklets had introduced me to my savior, the God who would deliver me from evil and fear, the God who would bless my efforts with success and happiness and reveal to me the basic truths of the universe. Despair and foreboding were to be replaced with comfort and expectant delight. Good news, right? Well, not exactly. It turned out there was a great deal of confusion about who this God was. There were bitter battles to be fought. I would see minds wither. Mine almost did.

But it wasn't that way at first. I was accepted at Ambassador College in Big Sandy, Texas—Armstrong's college, "God's college." I was thrilled to be there. I'd been *chosen*. And not by some mere admissions committee, but, I was told, by God Himself. I arrived on campus in August 1970, and soon after wrote these words in my journal: "I'm just another lost and lazy, disillusioned clod who came stumbling out of the muck and mire of the world into something so awesome and beautiful that his semi-perverted mind can't even fully grasp it."

I had found (or been found by) an organization in which to lose myself—the self that was troubled by doubt and anxiety. I was now part of an "army" that was the spearhead of the Kingdom of God; I was of the elite. Ambassador College was referred to as "the West Point of God's Work." The "Work" was what we were doing— spreading the gospel of Jesus Christ before the End Time, which was imminent. Garner Ted's father, Herbert, the founder of the Worldwide Church of God (WCG) and Ambassador College (AC), had written a sobering pamphlet entitled "1975 in Prophecy." This luridly illustrated tract proved to my satisfaction that the Second Coming of Christ would occur in less than five years. Members of each new freshman class at AC speculated on the odds of their graduating before the Great Tribulation, the three and one-half years of global anguish prophesied in the Book of Revelation. The greater part of mankind would die—violently. (Herbert's booklet featured a haunting picture of corpses being buried with a bulldozer.) During that time the WCG would flee to the Place of Safety, a desolate spot near Petra in the Negev Desert in Jordan, about fifty miles south of the Dead Sea. While the rest of the wicked world was horribly punished by means of war, famine, plagues, and natural disasters beyond imagining, we would hide and watch, waiting for Christ to descend upon the Mount of Olives in Jerusalem (Zech. 14:1-4). Then we'd be transformed into supernatural beings and help Him clean up the world, ushering in the Kingdom, God's own theocracy over the entire planet (and the rest of the universe).

While many of my generation were training for combat in the paddies, jungles, and hills of Southeastern Asia, I was training for the Battle of Armageddon, for spiritual combat with Satan and his minions. Some of our teachers believed we would engage in actual fighting—an ethereal, supernatural war against evil spirits. I always pictured it in terms of science-fiction fantasies—with flaming swords, thunderbolts, and God's own lasers. Years later, upon seeing *Star Wars*, I was struck with a vivid sense of deja vu. Actually, it sounded like a hell of a good time—a phantasmagoric, cosmic shootout with God on our side. We wouldn't have thought of it in such terms, but what we were anticipating was *Jihad*, a holy war in which we would slay the infidel and then rule the world as princes and priests of the Almighty God (Rev. 3:21, 5:10). Years later, I had no trouble understanding the Ayatollah Kohmeini's Revolutionary Guards. Fundamentalists, no matter what the particular religion, are more alike than different.

But meantime, back in East Texas, we were to lead lives pleasing to God in a manner revealed to us by the Armstrongs. AC was to be a showcase for how the earth would be after the Second Coming. Our lives, completely circumscribed by the Law of God, from the Ten Commandments to the priestly legislation in the Book of Leviticus, were to be shining examples to the world. We were to be the proof of God's transcendent pudding, the ultimate human products of enlightenment via obedience and submission to the precepts of the Holy Bible—as expounded (and expanded) by the Armstrongs.

The official motto of AC was "Recapture True Values." The student handbook asserted that we were being "afforded the opportunity of acquiring true knowledge and guidelines. In all the history of man, few have ever had the opportunity you are receiving. This is your CHANCE!! . . . The goal of Ambassador College is to teach you how to live." Our conduct was to be a refacimento of the Bible—directed and choreographed by the organization.

We received direction not only in precepts of morality, but in the physical, practical minutiae of daily life. More often than not, the physical seemed to take precedence over the spiritual. But I suppose that's normal in an army. Bodies are more easily disciplined than minds, and, if one rigorously trained the former, control of the latter might follow. The military has known this for centuries. For example, historian William H. McNeill, in his book *The Pursuit of Power*, wrote that military drill proved its efficacy in producing cohesive units of men:

"For when a group of men move their arm and leg muscles in unison for prolonged periods of time, a primitive and very powerful social bond wells up among them. . . . The feats of arms that European armies routinely performed, once drill had become soldiers' daily

experience, were in fact quite extraordinary. . . . Consider how amazing it was for men to form themselves into opposing ranks a few score
yards apart and fire muskets at one another, keeping up while com-
rades were falling dead and wounded all around. Instinct and reason
alike make such behavior unaccountable. Yet European armies of
the eighteenth century did it as a matter of course."

There was no parade ground at AC, and we didn't drill as such,
but we were directed what to wear, what and how to eat, when to
study, when to sleep, who to date and how often; we learned how,
when, and where to relax, pray, and read, and how to wear our hair,
ad infinitum. We "marched" onward in a lock step of social and
cultural conformity.

Few of these things were bad for us per se—there's nothing
wrong with a healthful diet, neat clothes, or a regular schedule. It's
only that they were *enforced*. Not as the mere guidelines and rules
of an educational institution, but as the will of God. A sloppy appearance at AC was not just an exercise in poor taste, it was rebellion
against God (and the Armstrongs). Freshmen were quickly enmeshed in a net of regulations, steeped in a comprehensive code of
behavior that considered nothing too trivial to scrutinize and critique.
Little of this code was actually graven in stone. Rather it was like an
oral Talmud, a tradition of past pronouncements, opinions, and
examples conveyed to new arrivals by the words and deeds of instructors, ministers, upperclassmen, and the very tone of the AC
environment. No one stood with a whip to beat freshmen into conformity. It was far more subtle, and hence far more effective. A
seemingly innocuous statement in the student handbook sums up
the attitude: "Notice what the *leading* upperclassmen wear and use
their standard as a *basic* guide. They will usually set the proper
example."

As in any army, our paramount lesson was respect for authority—unquestioning obedience to superiors. God was our commander-
in-chief, but he had divinely appointed the Armstrongs as His all-
powerful lieutenants, and they in turn had designated other men as
theirs. The church hierarchy was formal and rigid, with actual ranks
within the ministry and a clear pecking order for the rest.

For example, if a student wished to plan a social function, the
student handbook advised that "if your plans include a number of
other students, you should present your idea to the Dean of Students.
Individually organized cookouts, camp-outs, sing-alongs, or the like
should always be checked with Mr. Kelly." It wasn't that Kelly was
going to deny anyone, he just wanted to be asked—to have people
dependent upon him and subject to his final word. Once the superiors
had been established by appeal to the authority of God, there was
no need of force.

Once, during a student assembly, the Deputy Chancellor at Big Sandy mentioned that he was a fan of Louis L'Amour's western novels. Within weeks, the men's dormitories were inundated with L'Amour paperbacks. If there was any male then present at AC who didn't read at least one of those westerns, I never heard about it. (I managed one-and-a-half.)

"Ambassador," said the Student Manual, "is widely noted for its efficient, smooth-running student body. A large share of credit must go to its student officers. . . . They are not the 'gestapo' or faculty 'spies.'" That had to be said, of course, because it was precisely what many of them were. This semiofficial chain of command and control is what led to my first disillusionment with "the Work" and "God's College."

I entered the WCG and AC flush with hope and idealism. We were preparing the way for the return of Jesus Christ to end all pain and suffering in the world. It was heady wine, sometimes the source of an actual physical rush. I was ready to obey and conform, and I did. This was good for me, and I was good for the world. Doubt crept in slowly, nearly always squelched by the overwhelming presence of so many people doing, saying, and thinking the same things. Toeing the line was supposed to make us happy, and when people know they're *supposed* to be happy—that unhappiness is the result of sins against God—then they *act* happy, even if they're not. Who was I to doubt the word of God (and the Armstrongs) as exemplified by all the smiling faces of four hundred fellow students and seekers after righteousness? Could smiles be pernicious? Who was I to criticize the lieutenants and representatives of the Creator?

But did I really believe I needed to ask Mr. Kelly's permission to have fun? Or more importantly, did I really believe that all my friends and family back home—those apparently uncalled by God—were sinful, wretched, and caught up in the carnal machinations of an essentially evil world? Could I fully accept the notion that some of them might be cast alive into the Lake of Fire, exterminated forever because of their sins? Was I really a superior, consecrated person who would eventually serve as their ruler and model? (If they survived the "Wrath of God.") Was I happy with all that? And if I was unhappy, it was due of course to sin. To question the wisdom and authority of my superiors was a transgression of the Law of God. I strove to be happy.

But in early 1972, a minister named Howard Clark was transferred to Texas from the headquarters campus in Pasadena, California. He was something of a legend in the WCG. While serving with the Marine Corps in Korea, he was severely wounded and subsequently paralyzed. He received a one hundred percent disability from the Veteran's Administration and was confined to a wheelchair. But then "God called him into the Work," as we liked to say, and after being anointed with oil and prayed over by a WCG minister, he was healed—he was able to walk. He attended AC and rose through the ranks, demonstrating a remarkable talent for preaching and public speaking. It was said that during one sermon he vividly portrayed the story of David and Goliath by running up a step ladder to play the part of the giant. Another time he hauled a side of beef into the meeting hall and then flailed it with a whip, graphically demonstrating the sufferings of Jesus. He was loud and irreverent, articulate and keenly intelligent. One had to wonder why he was allowed to stay; he did little obeisance to sacred cows.

The presence of such a renegade was a revelation, but Clark offered us more than his mere puzzling existence. That summer, when life on campus slowed and many students and faculty were gone, he initiated what he called "waffle shops." These were informal evening gatherings advertised by word of mouth. There might be poetry readings (of all things!), a film, Bible study, and of course listening to Clark as he "waffled"—extemporaneously expounding on just about everything. To cadets in the army of God, regimented in body and spirit, this could be shocking.

During one waffle shop, Clark quipped: "If Jesus Christ was a student at AC today, we'd kick him out." We had strayed too far from the original precepts to be able to tolerate the original teacher. It was that heretical thought, and a thinly veiled reference to some WCG ministers as "con artists," that spurred the "gestapo" into action. A senior who had attended the gathering, a *leading* upper-classman, went to Dean of Students Kelly the next day and reported what distressing things he had heard. The waffle shops were officially banned.

I was dismayed. After that last meeting my friend Gerry and I had stayed up almost all night, discussing the meeting. We had been deeply stimulated, intellectually sparked. Nothing quite like it had happened to us before at AC. Why was that bad? The AC Bulletin explicitly stated: "Students are rigorously encouraged to use their own minds to think, to question, to check up on doctrines, concepts, and philosophies, to search for proof before accepting any." Was that mere lip service to intellectual freedom? (AC was trying to please an accreditation committee at the time, and such an open-minded statement may have been designed to impress them.) Had the administration been so confident that we would see it their way that they felt it was safe to ostensibly support critical thought? Apparently so. In reality, examinations of orthodoxy were to be nipped in the bud. Yet Clark was not dismissed, just silenced for a while. I had heard stories of people who were invited to leave the WCG for tamer ideas than his. Were they afraid of him in some way? And what was that—*they*? For the first time I thought of the AC administration in terms of "we" and "they."

Unlike most of the faculty, Clark lived off campus, away from the bosom of the institution. Students began filtering out there, alone or in small groups, to sit in his office and listen. Rumors of an "heretical underground," a "free thought movement," began to circulate. People felt threatened. But Clark was not attempting to undermine AC. His main point was that we were all individauls before God and that we must truly cultivate independent minds. But that was not necessarily good for the cohesiveness of the army.

Still, we persevered. If the men in charge weren't perfect, it remained "God's college," and it could be improved from the inside. There was, after all, the Work to be done, and in the face of worldwide redemption and restoration, our differences seemed petty.

But the cracks in the edifice of trust continued to splay. In the fall of 1972, the start of my junior year, one of the new crop of freshmen dropped a bomb. Before the end of the first semester he quit college, disillusioned. The attrition rate at AC was always high, (usually involuntarily, due to violations of the pharisaical rules), but rarely did a student leave because of philosophical principles, and none had ever left a poem behind to explain. Copies were made and circulated, and chords were struck. (The library's photocopying machine proved to be indispensable in the propagation of "free thought," and it was eventually sealed by the administration, its use restricted to those with official permission.) The poem talked about "hypocrites," and "people running,/pretending they're caring," and "inner torment that barely slips out," but the line that stood out most prominently was: "minds that don't ask why."

Here was a person who had been on campus for barely two months and was able to decide it was all a sham—counterproductive, injurious, and not worth his time. What was the source of such certainty? He had passed judgement, written about his insights, and voted with his feet. Was it courageous, independent thought, or was it, as some said, demon-inspired rebellion? But I had known the man—he wasn't evil. Maybe, like me, he'd just read *Elmer Gantry*, Sinclair Lewis' classic condemnation of the religious opportunist. In any case, I was impressed . . . and alerted. What had he so clearly seen of which I was only dimly aware? I had noticed things at AC that were less than idyllic, but I had never considered leaving, separating myself from the cutting edge of God's millennial sword.

That is, not until about a month later. A reliable source reported to my friend Bill that the Deputy Chancellor had remarked in the faculty dining room: "We must get rid of all the doubters." Bill was distraught. Was this "recapturing true values"? He spoke of his "raped idealism," and we fed each other our misgivings about AC, wondering if we belonged there, and, if we didn't, were we failures? Where could we go? If "God's college" had fallen short of the mark, what was left? (Bill had made a heavy investment. When he joined the WCG, his parents had sent him to a psychiatrist.) We were so wired into the organization that even when disillusioned with its actions, we could see no alternative. The fundamentalist mindset fosters an attitude of: if not this, then nothing, if not the fundamental God, then the abyss. Late one night we made up our minds to leave, but in the morning we were back in class, trapped by our dependence, rationalizing our commitment by hoping for reform. This organization was the source of our salvation—temporal and eternal—and we couldn't bear the thought of returning to "the world."

But my mind soon took a decisive turn, and it began in a classroom. Bill stood up to ask a question in Theological Research, the third-year Bible class. He was genuinely puzzled, and politely (I thought) disputed the conclusion we were supposed to have reached as the result of completing a homework assignment concerning the canonization of the Bible. The instructor, a minister named Chapman, immediately bristled. I could actually see him stiffen, tensing up as if for physical battle. If he had been a dog, his hackles would've risen. An argument ensued, with Chapman not addressing Bill's question, but rather accusing him of arrogance and insubordination. Bill stated repeatedly that he wasn't challenging Chapman's authority (though the question by its very nature of course had) nor showing disrespect, but the irate instructor ridiculed him, demanding to know if he even believed the Bible. A few students told me later that they had grown increasingly bewildered, amazed at what they considered to be a serious overreaction by Chapman. They said that if Bill had walked out, they'd have followed. (There'd been many complaints about the class among students.)

But finally Bill decided to just shut up and sit down. He was shocked, genuinely perplexed by the vehemence and contempt of Chapman's reaction to what Bill considered a legitimate question. This public attack by a superior, an ordained minister of God, was so distressing that Bill felt the whole thing must've been his fault. That evening he went to Chapman's home and apologized. This humbling, magnanimous effort received a cold, "Well, you *should* apologize" response. There was no sense of warmth or conciliation, and absolutely no admission of at least partial wrong. Bill left angry and humiliated, violated once again. He believed that at "God's college" there should be some recourse, so he made an official appointment with Chapman through his secretary, and I asked if I could tag along. We discussed the "mission" at length and decided our purpose would be to respectfully inform Chapman that the majority of his students were dissatisfied with the way his course was run, and to propose some changes we felt would be beneficial. We believed the attitude of the class, especially after Bill's excoriation, was ugly and that Chapman should be aware of it.

Unfortunately, we weren't granted our audience for three long weeks. During that time rumors burgeoned. We heard that Bill and I were going to "give Chapman hell." Clark called me into his office, curious about our intentions. I assured him we intended to handle the meeting in a calm, dignified manner and that we sincerely wished for some positive change in the third-year Bible class. He said he would go to bat for us if necessary.

On a Friday evening in December, we finally entered Chapman's office, nervous and intimidated. But he received us warmly, and we launched into our spiel. We requested an end to rote memorization of unimportant details, an entire textbook instead of the outline of one (we were using the framework of a thesis on canonization, which had been produced by an AC faculty member), a more tolerant handling of questions (we quoted the college bulletin), and an additional textbook—one produced outside the WCG—so we could obtain an overview of the topics covered. We spent two hours discussing these matters, and all was serene and friendly, at least on the surface. We shook hands as we left, and Bill and I were satisfied that all had gone well. We congratulated each other, convinced we had accomplished some good. Silly boys.

Next morning at Sabbath services, Chapman delivered the sermon. The standard length of a sermon in the WCG was one to two hours (though I sat through some as long as three, and heard about a few legendary five-hour marathons). Chapman all but personally attacked Bill and me for nearly an hour and a half. I was stunned. Bill had opted for the afternoon services and thus missed another public thrashing. In a vicious assault upon those who question and doubt, Chapman referred to several points we had discussed only several hours before in the apparently benign atmosphere of his office. I expected to hear our names spewed out at any moment, held up as pariahs or perhaps as insidious dupes of Satan. He set up straw men and violently knocked them down, quoting extensively from an outside theological work, which was obviously sloppy and in error as far as his audience was concerned. He used the book as an intellectual scapegoat, a means to ridicule contemporary scholarship in general (and hence *thinking* in general). He lambasted and belittled those who critically examined what he billed as *the Truth*. He laid it right out, asserting clearly, without equivocation: "IT'S NOT YOUR PLACE TO QUESTION WHAT YOUR TEACHERS TELL YOU!" So there it was—the true face of AC and the WCG. The hierarchy was not after truth, but power. They *had* all truth; there was no need to seek more. And there was especially no need to take any guff from mere students—lowly sheep of the flock.

At first I was livid, so angry and offended that my impulse was to leap up in the midst of Chapman's tirade and deliver one of my own. But that, of course, would only prove that I *was* rebellious, contentious, and proud—a sinner, and all that Chapman said I was. I shouldn't descend to his level, I told myself. For in spite of his condemnation, I still believed in the Work as a whole. I still desired to have a part in it. I hoped Chapman was merely a single rotten apple that wouldn't spoil the barrel.

Next day I walked into Clark's office, and he smiled and said, "Well, what are you going to do, run off screaming into the night, or laugh about it?" We laughed—there didn't seem to be anything else to do. I gave up on Chapman. Bill gave up on the institution. He opted for an early graduation the following spring, and went home to Ohio. He took his "raped idealism" and a heavy load of skepticism back out into "the world." I assumed he would leave the WCG for good. But he kept attending church services in Ohio, and once away from the brewing controversy at AC, his mind slipped back into the grasp of the organization. Later, after I had finally severed myself from the Armstrongs, I wrote to Bill to see where his mind was. He treated me gently and politely, but definitely as the pariah Chapman had thought us both to be. I never discovered what lulled him back into the all-encompassing womb, but it was as if my old friend had died. I never heard from him again.

In the meantime, we were buying books—under the counter. Clark had recommended *The Faith of a Heretic* by Walter Kaufman, and one of the students who worked at the college commissary ordered a few copies and kept them discreetly out of sight, far from the Louis L'Amour westerns. If someone specifically requested a copy, he would slip it into a bag and quietly hand it over. The eyes of the true believers were everywhere; this was not an acceptable book for God's students.

On page twenty-two, Kaufman had written: "The aim of a liberal arts education is not to turn out ideal dinner guests who can talk with assurance about practically everything, but people who who will not be taken in by men who speak about all things with an air of finality. The goal is not to train future authorities, but men who are not cowed by those who claim to be authorities."

These were not words that Chapman would have us memorize, especially since one of the conceits of AC was that it was providing us with a liberal arts education. My friend Gerry, who was on the staff of the college newspaper, once neglected to perform some small task that the faculty adviser expected him to have done.

"I thought [so and so] was going to do it," Gerry told the man.

"That's your problem," replied the journalism instructor/ordained minister, "you *think!*" He then told Gerry that he wanted him to be a robot, and, to demonstrate, he walked stffly and jerkily around the room. It was a sincere performance, devoid of irony.

"He who is fortunate, let him learn pain."

Schiller

Patrick Dwyer

The Bones of the Righteous

As I reviewed my life at God's College, I saw a richness in the texture of my experience—due partly to the impetuosity of youth, and partly to my inner resistance to mandated conformity. Some adventures at AC, however, were accidental; at least one was spectacular. But spectacular isn't necessarily pleasant.

It was a moment of abject, gut-churning terror. I was convinced I was going to die, smashed to a sickening pulp beneath three tons of hurtling steel. For a few seconds there seemed no alternative. My mind went blank, filled by a soundless scream that paralyzed all hope. I agonized in a dreadful anticipation of crushing, bloody pain.

I hadn't expected the day to be dangerous. There were no premonitions of disaster over morning coffee. I was going to work at the college water treatment plant. It was a pleasant fiefdom where I'd landed just by accident during my freshman year. It was the ideal campus job. My boss and I were the only two operators, and the work was so specialized that no one in the administration knew what we were doing, and therefore couldn't intrude. As long as clear water flowed from the taps it was assumed that all was well. I could study in the comfortable office while on shift, had access to a company

vehicle and was one of the few students who left that Bible school
with a readily marketable skill.

But like any complex processing or manufacturing, it was a high-
maintenance operation, and early in the afternoon one of our gas
heaters quit. It hung just below the twenty-foot ceiling of the plant,
a monstrous gray box enmeshed in a network of piping and conduit.
The boss inspected the unit from the top of a shaky ladder and decided that the heater required a serious cleaning and perhaps an
organ transplant or two. However, such a project could not be effectively pursued from the rungs of a ladder, and he decided to borrow a fork-lift from the shipping and receiving warehouse. We could
slip a pallet over the forks to serve as a working platform and then
raise someone (me) up to the heater to do the dirty work. Sounded
good, in theory.

The warehouse was across campus, about a mile from the water
plant, and we left our pickup there and climbed aboard the fork-
lift. The boss eased into the driver's seat, and I perched atop the
engine housing, hanging onto the cage. The vehicle wasn't designed
for passengers, but the spot was comfortable enough. In retrospect,
it seems odd that I didn't follow the boss in our pickup; there was no
need for both of us to be aboard the fork-lift. But maybe since we
had been working together all day, we just naturally teamed up. Or
perhaps we were in the midst of a conversation that we needed to
continue. Or probably it just looked like a fun thing to do.

In any case, I was astride the back of the fork-lift when we
reached the crest of Heartbreak Hill. I'd forgotten about it. The long,
steep grade had earned its name by being part of the running course
for physical education classes. From the fork-lift—a slow, cumbersome device intended for flat and benevolent warehouse floors—the
plunging hill looked suddenly ominous, like the start of a rapids or
the edge of a cliff. I could see the boss had forgotten about it too. I
saw his back stiffen as he pressed the brake.

We started to creep down the hill, but either the brakes were
worn or they weren't designed to hold the fork-lift on such a precip-
itous slope. The average warehouse, after all, doesn't feature a "Heartbreak Ramp." The machine gradually picked up speed, overriding
the brakes and the boss, and I could see he was losing control. As
the fork-lift started to fishtail, I rose to a crouch and considered
jumping off. But we were going twenty to thirty miles per hour and
the pavement looked terribly hard and unforgiving. I had a brief
vision of my skinned, scraped body skidding down the hill into the
path of an oncoming truck. Still, the fork-lift seemed bent on a suicide
run, and I tensed to leap when it all became academic.

The boss told a reporter later, "It got to zigzagging from one
side of the hill to the other, and I never could straighten it up." So

just before I was going to abandon ship, he decided to steer it into the brush. It seemed better to get off the road than risk running into another vehicle or reaching an even more frightening velocity. He spun the wheel and we hit the curb, shooting for the grass and trees. The machine bounced, and the forks speared into the ground. The fork-lift was catapulted through the air and I was flung off, my fearful grip ripped free of the cage. I was falling toward a patch of ground at the base of a large oak, and I could sense the tons of steel following close behind. I knew the fork-lift was going to land on me, and I *knew* I was going to be killed.

And so an instant later I was cosmically relieved to know I was only seriously injured. I felt the top of the fork-lift's cage crash down on my right ankle and foot. It pounded them into the ground and then rebounded and came to rest a few inches away. I think I cried out—loudly. I didn't actually hear bone shatter, but I realized it had. The ankle swelled up instantly, filling my boot to bursting. The pain was astonishing.

In a moment the boss was at my side, unlacing the boot. Amazingly, he'd been thrown clear of the cage with nothing more than bruised ribs and crushed pride. He was mortified. The fork-lift had been his idea. (The ladder, after all, would have been unsafe.) But of course I should never have ridden the back of the machine in the first place, and I was simply overjoyed to be alive and have him untie that boot. It didn't ease the pain, but it was a good boot and I didn't want someone to cut it off later. It's wondrous what banalities pass through the mind when it's torn between euphoria and agony. Profound observations would come later.

Other people appeared, and I was helped into the back-seat of a passing car and rushed to the college infirmary. In a tortured jiffy the boot was off. ("Don't lose that boot," I grated anxiously from between locked teeth.) Our local doctor took one look and called ahead to the hospital.

Since this was Ambassador College, a minister duly appeared to pray over me and anoint me with oil. It was a pleasant formality, a rote ritual. Nobody really expected me to rise off the table and walk. But a few words with God couldn't hurt, and as the minister prayed aloud he mentioned something that caught my attention. He said, "And may his present anguish and suffering help him to more fully appreciate the sufferings of his savior Jesus Christ." Hmm. I thought about that (later). What if a booming voice called to me from the sky: "Peter," it would say, "have I got a deal for you! You can save the world. All you've got to do is lie on the ground while I drop a three-ton fork-lift on your ankle. What do you say?" Well, let me think about it. (Later, couching this thought in more reverent terms, I revealed it to a pious coed I was trying to impress. I tacitly passed it off as an example of my deep, spiritual turn of mind in the presence of extreme adversity. I think she bought it.)

Back in the car, stretched out crosswise on the seat, I was absorbed by a terrific throbbing. Just before we left for the hospital, Dean of Students Kelly stuck his head in the window. He had heard one of his charges had screwed up in a big way. He peered at me for a moment and then said the only thing that came to him.

"Does it hurt?"

My brain leaped in confusion. Here was one of those moments when someone says something so outrageously vulnerable to a devastating wisecrack, that there's no way you can come up with one wise enough. I couldn't think of anything sufficiently sharp and sarcastic to do justice to such a query.

"Yeah," I replied. Another ripe moment lost forever.

The radio was on in the car, and I have a vivid recollection of hearing Hugo Montenegro's instrumental "The Good, the Bad, and the Ugly." The latter two summed up the twenty-four-mile ride to the hospital, but it was only the beginning of sorrows.

Properly posing for the X-rays rivaled the accident itself. (We need to have the ankle *this way!*) The pictures showed that I had a fracture of the tibia; the lower leg was broken in two places, the end of the bone was cracked completely off and "floating" free. The orthopedic surgeon said it would have to be refastened with a screw. Whatever; go for it.

I was wheeled to a room, flopped onto a bed and lay there fully clothed. I assumed surgery would get underway forthwith, but six hours later a nurse peeked in and asked—somewhat irritably—if I'd called my parents yet. (My mother was in Minnesota; I was in Texas.) I was only twenty years old, and the hospital needed permission other than mine to operate.

Well, no, I hadn't thought of that. She fetched me a pair of crutches and I hobbled to the pay phone at the nurses' station. I bummed a dime from the woman on duty and made a collect call. Trying to keep the torment out of my voice, I said, "Hey Mom, how's it going? . . . yes, fine, fine . . . well, no, ah, you see I've got a little problem here . . . no, I'm in a hospital and the doctor needs your permission to fix my broken leg . . . naw, it's no big deal, a little accident . . . I'm okay . . . no, no, it doesn't hurt too bad, that was ah, ah someone across the hall . . . thanks Mom, tell it to the doctor." Then I struggled back to my room and lay there for another thirty hours. I guess they figured: what the hell, he's not *going* anywhere.

Finally I was wheeled into surgery where they stuck a hypo the size of a knitting needle into my wrist, and the next thing I knew I was lying back in bed. My leg was in a cast from toes to crotch, and it still hurt like hell. They injected the appropriate drugs, but the effects wore off in minutes—or so it seemed. I tried reading. I got about a hundred pages into a western novel, right up to the point where the hero falls off a cliff and breaks his leg. I almost threw up.

That evening I got a roommate. A jovial man in his mid-forties was eased into the next bed. He was sporting a cast identical to mine and had also sustained a fracture of the tibia.

"How'd yours happen?" he asked, using the passive voice. Such grammar is common to victims of all stripes. We generally assume we had little or nothing to do with our own misfortunes. Some capricious or malevolent *deus ex machina* had it in for us.

I launched into my harrowing tale of the wild, runaway forklift, and as I proceeded with my exaggerations, I saw his face take on a sheepish cast.

"How'd yours happen?" I asked.

He gave a rueful snort. "I slipped on a rug in my damn kitchen!" I could see he was a good sport, so I laughed uproariously. "Hey," he said, "there's a juice call at 9:00 p.m. Order orange juice."

"Why?"

"Never mind. Just order OJ."

At around 9:00 a nurse came in, and we both requested orange juice. After it was delivered, my companion slipped a bottle of vodka from under his pillow. Gleefully chortling like a couple of teenagers, we mixed screwdrivers (light on the orange juice) until we were both half-in-the-bag. Then he hit the emergency call button next to his bed and started yelling, "Nurse! Nurse!"

In an instant she burst through the door and cried, "What is it!"

"We need more sheets! We need more sheets!"

"Why?" she demanded.

He gestured widly at our second-story window.

"Because," he gasped, "if we tie the ones we've got together, they won't reach the ground!"

She cursed and left.

It was the high point of my nine-day hospital stay. Other than much-appreciated visitors (one horde of sympathetic Bible students grew so loud that the duty nurse sent a security guard to the room. We were holy, but we knew how to raise hell) the only other bright spot was the name a nurse had inadvertently printed on my hospital bracelet: MESCHAK. You said it.

I left the hospital like a man reborn, but I wasn't quite delivered. The awful pain had largely subsided, but the full-length cast remained, and the inevitable itching began. It started as a minor irritation and I told myself to ignore it—don't focus on it, and it'll go away. Sure. Soon the itching was pervasive. It filled my nervous system, and I lay in bed paralyzed, imagining ants and ticks. I violently twisted my leg the full quarter-inch it would move. I banged on the cast with a broom handle. I tried clawing at my right armpit, hoping for a sympathetic reaction in the depths of the cast. It was all for nought. My mind grew perverse.

After a full day of insidious torture, I grabbed a metal coat hanger and bent it straight. Hook first, I shoved it deep into the cast, down to the spot where the teeming ants seemed to be concentrated. Gingerly, I started to scratch. Oh man! I went faster, digging harder, in and out, in and out. Oh wow! I hit my stride, scratching furiously—overwhelmed by intense relief. I worked the hanger until my leg hurt. The itching was replaced by a sharp, tearing pain. Good. That I could handle.

For the next three days I roughly wielded the hanger, transforming the maddening itch into plain old bearable pain. Sometimes it emerged with bits of skin clinging to the hook, but anything was better than the itching. And then I began to detect a foul odor emanating from the cast. It was a putrid, rotting kind of smell. Fearing infection, but fearing the hospital more, I decided to treat it myself. I found a bottle of Jade East cologne and noted the high alcohol content. I dumped it down the cast, and it nearly blasted me through the roof. For several minutes, I felt as if my leg was on fire, but in the end the wound was treated and the cast smelled a lot better. Strangely, it didn't itch for a long time. I wondered if the cologne people would be interested in a paid testimonial. "Jade East Cologne: for the *big* sweetening jobs."

Actually, I was probably lucky I didn't get gangrene and lose the leg—though amputation would certainly have taken care of the itching problem and seemed like a viable alternative at the time. No doubt my doctor would've been horrified to learn of my coat hanger-cologne procedure, but in the end he nailed me with something almost as tacky.

It was nine months later. The cast was long since off, and it was time to extract the two-inch stainless steel, self-tapping screw that had held my tibia together. I had been given the option of leaving it in forever, perhaps a curio for some future archaeologist, but the surgeon strongly hinted that it would probably be better to take it out—minor surgery, local anesthetic. Maybe he needed a little easy money.

In any case, he convinced me, and I felt fairly comfortable about the operation until I saw his three surgical instruments lying in a sterile tray next to the table: a scalpel, a Phillips screwdriver, and a ball-peen hammer. It looked like equipment needed to perform a little warranty work on Frankenstein.

Still, it seemed to go smoothly (he used the hammer to set the screwdriver—the anesthetic just barely handled it), and soon he held up my souvenir screw, then sewed me back together with twenty professional-looking stitches.

I'd brought along a pair of rental crutches, figuring I'd have to hop around for a few days. The doctor was amused to see that some campus wags had customized them with a felt-tip pen. One crutch read: Olympic Fork-lift Team. The other featured a verse from the Book of Psalms: "The bones of the righteous shall not be broken." But after surgery the doc said: "You won't need those. Just lie here for twenty minutes, then walk out."

I threw in an extra ten, and a half-hour later I waltzed out of there. When I got back to my dorm I felt a strange squishing in my shoe. I pulled it off to find it full of blood—I could literally *pour* it out. All twenty stitches had come apart. Well, that tore it (so to speak). The surgeon had blown his credibility. Encouraged by my success with Jade East, I decided to treat the wound myself. I crammed the gaping fissure full of an antiseptic cream and slapped a gauze pad over it. Then pinching the wound closed as much as possible, I wrapped it several times (tightly) with duct tape. I ignored it for ten days. There's a nifty scar, but otherwise it healed up just fine.

And, yes, the whole affair did give me a greater appreciation for the sufferings of Jesus Christ. And of everyone else too. Such experiences are instructive. And I didn't ruin that boot. But there is one thing I do regret: I wish that nurse had brought us more sheets.

"Time it was,
And what a time it was,
It was . . .
A time of innocence,
A time of confidences.
Long ago . . . it must be . . .
I have a photograph.
Preserve your memories;
They're all that's left you."

Paul Simon
Bookends

Mark Coyle

Photogenic King Lear

With so many teachers attempting to teach us so much, there was bound to be an occasional triumph in the struggle for education. Sometimes even a classroom lecture can be the source of an influential thought. For example: "Your best friend is the garbage can."

Thus spoke one of my first instructors in photography. He was urging us to be critical of our work, to be unafraid of shoving a thumb through a substandard slide or cumpling a mediocre print. I took this admonition to heart, and over the years I've consigned thousands of emulsions to well-deserved oblivion.

There are many factors, technical and aesthetic, that separate good photos from bad. Any photographer worth his halide can ramble on to the point of ennui about contrast, grain, and depth of field, composition, and how these variables pertain to the particular photo being examined. Yet many of the pictures found in drawers, wallets, albums, and even portfolios are critically deficient in one or several technical and/or artistic categories, but they haven't been trashed. There are two reasons for this universal accumulation of photographic dross: 1) most people haven't run across my photo instructor, and no matter how putrid their pictures might be, they cost money, and 2) even if a certain shot is not up to the specs of an Ansel Adams, it possesses a personal significance for its creator.

Even a former would-be craftsman such as I, who was groomed (unsuccessfully) to be a professional and was drilled relentlessly in the extermination of inferior negatives (emulsive eugenics), have a few of *those* kind of pictures hidden away. They aren't retained for the sake of art, but rather for the memories they represent. For instance, I keep one embarrassingly lousy print that my old teacher would have destroyed instantly—remorselessly. It's a grainy, poorly focused, underexposed shot of a cowboy on a horse. I don't know the cowboy, but the horse's name was King Lear. He was a bucking bronco, a wild rodeo attraction, and one warm summer night in Texas he tried to kill me.

I was a staff photographer for the Ambassador College newspaper and yearbook. It was fun, but our assignments didn't always provide ideal opportunities for snapping Pulitzer contenders. The same events in the same settings with many of the same faces had been dutifully documented year after year for a decade. One could thrill to only so many images of the local version of Wilt the Stilt going up for two at the Big Game. Be it 1964 or 1994, a win or a loss, the photographs were essentially interchangeable. In a quest for something different, I once recorded a star player digging in his crotch out on the court (infernal jock strap!), and while my editors were amused, the print never saw the light of a copy camera.

So I was always alert for a new angle on an ancient subject, or better, a new subject. When I heard a rodeo was coming to the area I was excited. Here was a fresh challenge, a respite from portraits of "the secretary of the week" and nerve-racking faculty mug shots. A rodeo! Here was action, drama, color, danger.

Armed with a twin-lens Yashica D camera and a Matador flash unit with power pack—I could fry retinas at sixty feet—I headed for the small outdoor arena in Gladwater, Texas. The night air was charged with anticipation and the aroma of manure, and the wooden, whitewashed bleachers were packed with noisy rodeo fans. The fun had already started by the time I arrived, and my pulse rate heated up as I saw a wantonly careening Brahman bull fling a rider into the mud. The cowboy scrambled to his feet and slopped rapidly for the fence, the frantic, high-kicking bull lurching after him. As a clown dashed in to distract the beast, I noticed a flurry of activity in one corner as a small herd of photographers scampered for safety. With a glinting and glittering of polished metal and glass, they were up and over the fence and poised for more shooting. There was my niche.

I slipped through the crowd, climbed over the fence and eased into the mud. The gaggle of photographers had reentered the arena, and I joined them in the end near the chutes, awaiting the next rider.

As I posed there, primping my equipment and looking cooly professional for the benefit of the fans, I felt stabs of pain in my right ankle. The cast had come off only three weeks earlier, and my ankle was still a little swollen. Fractured three months before, it wasn't quite back to normal. I tried to forget about it and concentrate on rodeo photography.

The public address system crackled, and the emcee drawled out the next event: the bareback broncs. As the first horse and rider were announced, the photographers advanced farther out into the arena and focused on the chute. An angry bronc was banging against the boards as a cowboy gingerly attempted to climb aboard its thrusting back. I planted myself to one side of the group, estimating distance, pre-focusing, and making sure my flash unit was charged.

With a violent surge of pent-up fury, the bronc burst from the chute, and we all blasted away until the rider was thrown. The horse charged off to the other end of the arena where it was headed off and driven back into a chute by two riders on more docile mounts. I had managed to squeeze off two shots during the brief struggle, but I knew they were inadequate. I didn't have a telephoto lens, and I realized I had been too far from the subject. In order to glean anything decent enough to escape the garbage can, I'd have to close in on the action. Besides, I was conscious of the crowd. There were several friends and acquaintances in the stands, and I wanted to look professional. I had a romantic view of photographers, nurtured by the exploits of Robert Capa and David Douglas Duncan. Of course Capa had died violently in Indochina in the process of glorification, but that only served to embellish his reputation. So as the daring photographers prepared for the next bronc, I edged further out into the arena, in front of the rest. I adopted a stance that I believed made me appear both cool and expertly alert, all the while glancing sideways at the bleachers, trying to locate familiar female faces. I caught the tail of the announcer's introduction, ". . . riding King Lear!" I was amused at this touch of Shakespearean class mingling with ten-gallon hats and "shit-kickers."

King Lear exploded from the chute. I pressed my eye to the "sport-finder" peep sight of my Yashica and took a shot. In the blaze of the powerful Matador the action was frozen for an instant on my eyeball. King Lear, all four hooves off the ground, had his back hunched upward in the classic bronco pose. His rider, dressed all in white and flying high above the perilous muck, wore a mask of grim concentration. Good! But they were still too far away. I ventured a few steps closer, but King Lear veered toward the far side of the arena and flung the cowboy from his back. Immediately the two outriders charged in to corral him, and the show was apparently over.

I turned away (cooly) and started to amble toward the other

photographers, still dissatisfied. I was studying the ground, skirting some particularly evil mud, when a bustle of activity caused me to look up. My colleagues were about twenty yards away and rushing for the fence. Something was wrong. I whirled around and saw only horseflesh—the black head, broad chest, and pounding knees of King Lear. He was two strides away and closing, a blur of raging bronco. I didn't have time to budge. In an instant his right flank slammed me to the ground. He was over me and trampling. I watched in stunned fascination as one of his rear hooves came down with awesome force. It landed precisely on my recently fractured ankle, leaving a permanent hoof print in the leather of my boot. Only the cushioning effect of the soft mud saved the ankle from being rebroken. But I didn't know that at the time, and the pain made me gasp as my foot was literally hammered into the ground. Lear stomped me once, and then the riders had him, and he was soon back in the chute. But I knew how the *other* Lear felt, when, in the midst of the furious storm in Act III he mourned to Kent: "I am a man more sinned against than sinning."

I was also dazed, and not entirely cheery, as I struggled painfully to my feet and hobbled toward the fence. I was now an attraction in my own right, but this was not the sort of recognition I had been coveting. My flash unit was broken and dangling pitifully at my waist, my backside was caked with mud. I clambered awkwardly (and uncooly) over the fence and spent what seemed like an hour limping through the crowd. I endured dozens of amused smiles and mordant grins, humbly suspecting that I didn't even have a good negative to show for it all. Back at the college I phoned the campus doctor, a man who had seen me destroy two casts, and explained that I may have refractured the ankle. He hung up.

Nevertheless, my editor was entertained, receiving a detailed account of the farce from one of my "friends." He published my one lousy photo of King Lear and also ran a cartoon showing me being trampled. Accompanying this art was a subtly sarcastic story about my "coverage" of the rodeo. Well, it *was* something new, and it did manage to upstage "the secretary of the week." And everyone expressed relief that King Lear was unhurt.

And so this brutish image remains in my photo file. It should've been discarded, but I think my photography instructor would understand. My "coverage" was forgettable, but the memory of King Lear endures. After all, my friends and I were Texans then, and not only were we supposed to be soldiers of God, but we also felt compelled to be cowboys.

"It's better to know than not to know."

Walker Percy

Mark Coyle

Gunslingers' Progress

Gerry shot himself by mistake. The .22 long rifle bullet left the muzzle of his six-shooter before the gun fully cleared his holster. It ripped through the leather and into his thigh. He didn't realize until later that the slug tunneled the length of his leg and stopped in his calf. At the moment of impact he fell to the ground and bled.

He was practicing his "quick draw"—with live ammunition— but I wasn't one to criticize. A few weeks before, I'd gashed open my palm (the scar is still prominent) while attempting to "fan" my own pistol. The hammer simply stuck in my hand—embarrassing, not to mention painful. I should've known that the movie cowboys had been jiving me about manipulating a revolver into a machine gun.

We ostensibly bought our revolvers to kill rats. Gerry worked at Ambassador College's chicken ranch. (The institution took pride in self-sufficiently—preparing for the Millennium.) The chicken house was a haven for rodents, and once or twice a month, three or four of us gunslingers would force a showdown. We thought of it as public service. (Actually, we were just suckers for the macho allure of handguns.)

One of our party—determined by lot in authentic Old Testament fashion—would climb into the dingy, cob-webbed attic with a flashlight and his pistol. The tactic was to snap on the light and commence firing. In the sudden glare, the attic was thick with eyes and furry scuttlings. The rest of us stood on the floor below, our backs in a circle, our guns ready. In a moment, dozens of rats scurried down the walls, and we blasted away with abandon.

We managed to shoot a few rats (and a couple of innocent chickens), but considering the quantity of rounds being discharged, their casualties were low. I estimated that over the course of one winter we expended nearly a thousand .22 cartridges. Sections of the chicken house walls were as airy as a colander, and I was amazed we never got in trouble for this childish mayhem. But it was always a late-night activity, and the chicken house was isolated from the rest of the campus. Strangely, no one in authority ever mentioned the bullet holes.

So it was in the chicken yard where Gerry dropped with a bullet in his leg. He was alone. He felt the sickening onset of shock and was terrified that he was going to pass out and bleed to death. Inspired by this grim expectation, he stumbled and crawled several hundred yards to the adjacent golf course. Commandeering an unattended golf cart, he drove to our dorm, peeled off his clothes and collapsed in a shower stall. He was seen only by our friend Dave. It was summer, so most of the student body was gone, and our dorm was practically deserted. Dave got on the phone immediately—not to summon an ambulance, Gerry forbid it—but to call me.

I was in the office at the college's water treatment plant in the midst of some lab work.

"You better come to the dorm," he said.

"Why?" It was an unusual request in the middle of the day.

"Just come over here right now."

"But why? I'm busy."

Dave's voice turned strident. "Just get over here!" He hung up.

I finished a pH test and drove to the dorm. Gerry was lying in bed, racked with pain. Dave hovered over him helplessly. When Gerry told me what happened, my first impulse was to guffaw. What a ridiculous mishap! I shook my head. "Well, let's see it."

He pulled a towel away from his thigh, and I was bemused. I'm not sure what I expected a gunshot wound to look like, but certainly something more awesome and dramatic than this small, purple chicken butt. There was no hole per se, just a fleshy indentation, discolored and a little swollen. It looked like the anus of a white Leghorn. Gerry and I and a few others had once spent a long day butchering four hundred chickens at the ranch, and I was intimately familiar with every component of chicken anatomy. We had come away blood-stained and goofy after so much concentrated slaughter, and we offended everyone in the dining hall by brandishing severed chicken feet during the meal, making the toes clench and release by manipulating dangling tendons. The entre that evening was fried chicken. I couldn't face a bite, and neither could several others after we displayed our "marionettes."

"It looks like a Leghorn butt!" I exclaimed, and Gerry almost smiled through the pain. He tapped his calf and said, "Check this out."

The bullet felt like it was less than an inch beneath the surface— I could almost pinch it. I was incredulous. The slug had passed through Gerry's knee without doing any apparent damage. He could bend it with no discomfort. It was astonishing luck, but we attributed it to God. We were, after all, Bible students, and we remarked how merciful He must be to allow Gerry to survive such a ridiculous stunt. However, we weren't faith healers, at least not when it came to bullets.

"Well," I sighed, "let's get you to a doctor."

"No way!" Gerry grunted. "No way!" He explained how he'd thoroughly cleaned the wound in the shower and dosed it with iodine. He didn't need a doctor. What he required now was a painkiller, and that's where I came in. Would I please drive into town and buy him a couple of bottles of wine?

I was stupefied. "You've been shot!" I cried. "Don't be an idiot. We're taking you to the clinic."

But Gerry wouldn't have it, and we argued vociferously. His chief fear, it turned out, was public exposure. Once he sought medical aid, the cat was out of the bag, and he was utterly embarrassed by the episode. If word got out to the student body, he would never live it down. And there was the reaction of the administration to consider. The deans were autocratic and quick to chastise. "They'll take our guns away," Gerry warned.

That gave me pause. It was no doubt true, and Lord knew we loved our revolvers. The thought of forsaking our late-night shootouts at the chicken house was dismaying. I began to waver.

"Look at this chicken butt," Gerry said, indicating the wound with a dismissive wave, "Does that honestly look serious to you?" I had to admit that it did not.

As I think back, intrigued by our easy insouciance, I realize that this contempt for the flesh was the essence of youth. I haven't seen Gerry for several years, but I suspect if he shot himself in the leg today, dialing 911 would be his first priority—and to hell with embarrassment. By this time we've seen several friends and relatives pass on, and we sport too many aches and gray hairs to evade the substance of mortality. At age twenty it seemed our hard, pliant bodies couldn't betray us, and as Bible believers we enjoyed the added confidence of Holy Writ: ". . . in God I have put my trust; I will not fear what flesh can do unto me." (Ps. 56:4) But even our simple faith was a manifestation of youth; most adolescents trust in biology, if not in the Deity. I still have beliefs in early middle age, but they've been complicated by experience. I'm not nearly as smug or so carelessly brave as I used to be. "Young men," wrote George Chapman, "think old men are fools; but old men know young men are fools." Perspective is everything.

Thus it's incredible to me now, these many years later, that, after examining the "chicken butt," I drove to town and bought Gerry two or three bottles of Boone's Farm wine ("Koolade with a kick" we called it). He guzzled, till he was woozy and almost cheerful, and, with me as his dutiful "gopher," he remained somewhere between half-drunk and genuinely plastered for the next three days. ("Drink no longer water, but use a little wine for thy stomach's sake and thine often infirmities." I Tim. 5:23) After that his pain eased significantly. His total "medical" bill came to about ten dollars—it was cheap wine.

Dave and I vowed secrecy and were faithful. It was nearly a year before Gerry told anyone the story, and by then it had evolved into an uproarious anecdote; later it was legend. The vast majority of students (and *all* faculty) never found out. Gerry was spared general humiliation, and we kept our guns. We thought we were cool, of course, and I suppose it was true. But I sincerely hope I'm never that cool again. "For a living dog is better than a dead lion." (Eccles. 9:4)

"When you jump, it's just you."

US Army recruiting poster

Fred Yiran

A Passage
and A Parachute

Some church authorities frowned on extraordinary physical risk, said it was "tempting God," and we shouldn't engage in hazardous sport. But what exactly constituted such sport was a gray area. No one had suggested I not shoot the rodeo (though in retrospect such advice would've been wise), and many have ended up in casts as a result of a more or less civilized game of tennis. So I didn't worry much about what dangers God might or might not sanction. I had a more profound question:

When is a boy a man? At puberty? At age eighteen? When he lands a full-time job? (Many women, of course, would say "never.") It's more than academic. Our national sloppiness about the question has led to absurdities such as eighteen-year-olds who were not man enough to vote or drink, but man enough to fight and die in Vietnam. (The average age of U.S. combat troops in Indochina was nineteen.)

Many primitive cultures were more circumspect about developing a method for establishing official maturity. In *The Hero with a Thousand Faces*, Joseph Campbell writes:

"The so-called rites of passage, which occupy such a prominent place in the life of a primitive society . . . are distinguished by formal, and usually very severe exercises of severance, whereby the mind is radically cut away from the attitudes, attachments, and life patterns of the stage being left behind."

We fancy our civilization to be far beyond the primitive, but that doesn't mean that such heavy-duty rites have no value for us. Campbell continues:

"It has always been the prime function of mythology and rite to supply the symbols that carry the human spirit forward . . . in fact, it may well be that the very high incidence of neuroticism among ourselves follows from the decline among us of such effective spiritual aid."

We still need to know our place, and in the absence of an appropriate, traditional rite, individuals must seek their own passages to adulthood. We've ceased to think of it in cultural and/or tribal terms, but we all must prove ourselves in our early years, discovering where we stand.

At age twenty-one, when my verdant youth had reached a sort of critical mass, I decided I required a consciously performed rite of passage, a test of bravery and manhood. Actually, I determined I needed a series of tests, and one of them was to be a parachute jump. In many societies, a transition to maturity involved a trial of courage, and leaping from an undamaged, untroubled airplane seemed to fit the bill. Just the thought of it made me feel older. I'd heard that a small college in Arizona required a jump as part of freshman orientation, and I wanted to be so oriented. I wished I had gone to that college and been supplied with an institutionalized rite. Trepidation likes company.

Seeking support for my wavering determination, I linked up with three other young male students in the thrall of similar needs, and we made arrangements to jump. A simple phone call put us on the road to maturity. The man at the airfield told us there would be four hours of instruction and then he would "put you out at 3,500"—feet, that is.

So one cool evening in November 1972, we drove into Oklahoma and walked (a little uncertainly) into a tavern in the small town of Hugo. The joint was the unofficial headquarters of the Hugo Skydivers. The bartender was our instructor. After serving us a couple of Coors, he reached up over the bar and pulled down a set of roll-up charts. The first was a diagram of a parachute, and with a beer in one hand and a pointer in the other, he launched our initiation. I suddenly wished I hadn't downed that second brew. The bartender/jumpmaster was glibly rattling on about matters of life and death, and we perched on barstools, squinting at the most important pictures we had ever seen. I gripped the edge of the bar with sweaty palms and wondered, "What have we done?"

After an hour or so of intensive data input (we had all put a stop to the input of alcohol), the "classroom" phase of our training was complete. We retired for the evening, nervously exchanging second thoughts. But the morning dawned crisp and clear with light winds (a critical consideration), and we all nurtured a renewed sense of invulnerability. We arrived at the airfield alert and gung ho. The "lab" portion of our training began with "cut-aways." We learned that if our main chute malfunctioned, we must get rid of it before pulling the ripcord of the reserve chute, and perhaps save our lives. Dumping the main chute is called cutting away and has to be done in a matter of seconds by manipulating a pair of clips on the parachute harness. The exercise wasn't difficult, at least not on solid ground, and we proceeded quickly to the "PLF," or Parachute Landing Fall. This maneuver is designed to cushion the impact of returning to earth. It's a technique for hitting the ground and rolling that distributes the force over the entire body instead of just on the ankles and legs. To practice, we jumped off a four-foot platform into pea gravel. This quaint procedure was supposed to simulate an actual landing, and we believed it. Silly boys. We would be using military chutes and subsequently discovered what landing really was like: stand on the roof of a van and have it driven over rough terrain at ten to fifteen miles per hour; then jump off—backwards. Obviously, if the training was too authentic, many wouldn't make it to the actual jump. Here was one of those cases where a little ignorance was more than a little bliss.

After mastering the diluted PLF, we moved on to "aircraft exit form" (arms and legs spread wide and back hard-arched) and other key techniques, which were always presented as absolute truths and then qualified. We were told, for example, that if the airplane seems to be having mechanical troubles, stay with it! It's safer to stay inside than jump from an unstable plane. *However*, if the pilot beats you out the door . . .

After we were deemed to have passed the course, we watched one of the club members jump. The guy was a student himself, but had twenty-five jumps to his credit—just enough to make him stupid. We stared, spellbound, as he dropped out of the Cessna 172. He was a long way up, little more than a speck in the sky, but we could track him as he made a free fall that seemed to last forever. When his chute finally billowed open, I gasped in relief, realizing I hadn't been breathing. In a few minutes he came sailing over the drop zone, "flying" his chute in the breeze, and even we neophytes could tell he was being careless. The drop zone was only about a half mile from the local hospital and the high-voltage power lines that served it. The student jumper was headed directly for them.

"Where's he going?" someone asked in a brittle, fearful voice.

(I think it was me.)

A cynical veteran calmly replied, "To the hospital."

From our vantage the power lines were partially obscured by a small rise, and when the jumper hit the wires all we saw was a horrifying flash of electricity. There was a sickening zapping sound, and then we were running madly over the hill.

Shreds of his parachute were still burning on the wires, and we expected a charred corpse below, but the guy lucked out. He'd managed to slip between the powerlines and then cut away from his chute as it draped across the wires and flamed out over his head. He'd dropped about twenty feet to the ground and was there praying when we arrived. As soon as it was clear he would live, the rest of the club lashed into him with a harsh critique of his performance. A police car streaked toward the airfield; the hospital's power had been cut off, and I was given to understand it was the second time this had happened. A lot of people were upset, including my buddies and me. What sort of insanity was this? Well, we were soon to discover, for when the commotion died down, it was our turn to be "put out."

By means of an elaborate formula, which now escapes me, it was decided I should be first. As I climbed into the plane, Billy-Don, the jumpmaster, had a few encouraging words: "That exit form is the key. Do it right and you're okay; mess it up and you're fucked!" Gee, thanks, Billy-Don.

Since this was a first jump, the rip cord of my main chute was linked to a static line, which was secured to a ring set in the floor of the plane. When I jumped, the static line would deploy and automatically open my chute. Greenhorns can't be trusted to pull their own rip cords. Just a few months before we had read of a woman who'd been killed on her first jump. The jumpmaster had forgotten to hook her static line to the ring, and she'd neglected to make her own mandatory check, so she left the plane in a free fall. She still could have yanked a rip cord, but she never did. She had a mesmerizing, twenty-one-second fall to oblivion. (I once talked to a paramedic who had responded to such a mishap, and he said that curiously, there was little blood—and few bones. They had to "roll" the corpse into a body bag.)

Our altitude would be 3,500 feet, and it seemed to take hours for the Cessna to climb there. As the surface of the planet receded, I felt terror clutch my chest. I honestly feared I was going to wet my pants, or worse. For the first time, I faced the reality of what was happening. The training had been fun—playful and distracting— but now it struck me with painful intensity that there were only two ways out of this situation: I could actually *jump* from the aircraft, or I could face the crushing humiliation of returning to the ground with parachute intact. I finally and regretfully decided that death was preferable to ignominy, a decision that doubtless has sustained millions of young men in their test of manhood. I fervently prayed for courage and bowel control.

Then Billy-Don put his helmet close to mine and shouted above the blast of wind tearing through the open doorway of the plane, "*Think* about what you're going to do! *Hard-arch and count!*"

I nodded, and, as if by miracle, the fear evaporated. I had something to do. The count to which he referred was the six seconds we were to allow for free fall before the chute popped open. If it hadn't deployed in six seconds, it wasn't going to. I rehearsed the count over and over, like a comforting mantra: one-thousand-one, one-thousand-two, one-thousand-three. . . . My thoughts assumed the structure of a grade school arithmetic drill, evening out into a weird state of resigned tranquility. I wasn't going to mess in my jeans after all.

As we approached the final run over the drop zone (in our case, the target was a parachute laid out in a hay field), Billy-Don barked out the first command in the exit sequence: "Put your feet out!"

I rotated cautiously from my sitting position on the deck, remembering to keep my right hand covering the rip cord of my belly-mounted reserve chute. That was to prevent an "accidental deployment" inside the aircraft. If the wind caught a loose chute . . . I had been assured that being ripped through the fuselage was a lousy, tacky way to die. I then thrust my feet out the doorway and onto the narrow step on the side of the plane. The cold prop blast tore viciously at my pants legs.

"Get out on the strut!" Billy-Don yelled.

Keeping my left foot on the step and grasping the angled wing strut with both hands, I hung out over space with my right leg dangling free. I perched there beneath the wing of the plane, gazing down at an expanse of ludicrously tiny trees.

Then the final command. Billy-Don slapped me on the thigh and shouted, "Go!" I went. It was simple. I dropped off into nothingness.

I spread my limbs and arched my back, executing the critical move without difficulty. I was stable in the air. One of the main causes of parachute malfunction is a poor body position when the chute opens. Lines can get tangled and twisted, and a partially opened chute makes for a fast ride and a deadly landing.

The few seconds of free fall before the static line (4,000-pound test) opened my chute were ecstatic. Since nothing was going by, there was no sensation of falling, and I felt suspended in midair, weightless. It's exhilarating to look at the horizon from 3,000 feet up and have no sense of motion—seemingly free of the earth and a component of the sky itself.

Then, with a sudden tug and an abrupt shock, I was swinging

beneath the thirty-five-foot nylon canopy, watching the dwindling form of the Cessna, almost eye-level in the sky. I was surprised at the silence. It was radically quiet, a free and floating world of miniature landscape, hazy blue horizon, and endless firmament. I realized later that despite my rehearsal in the plane, I forgot to count. Many first jumpers do, overwhelmed by the grandeur. Fortunately the parachute hadn't been depending upon me.

Billy-Don jumped several seconds after I did, intending to guide me down by means of shouted instructions. But he didn't reach me in time, and as I wafted peacefully toward the earth, a man on the ground began calling out directions. At first I could only hear his voice and couldn't make out the words, but finally, after a minute more of "canopy ride" (it took about two-and-a-half minutes to descend), I heard him yelling, "Hold! Hold!" That meant I was to turn my chute into the wind. This would have a braking effect on my lateral velocity. The modified military cargo chute (T-10) I was using had a built-in ground speed of seven miles per hour. Up to that point I had been running before the wind and adding its speed to that of the chute. I was going too fast for a safe landing. (Though "safe landing" may be an oxymoron when dangling beneath an unforgiving T-10.) I pulled down on one of the two steering toggles hanging just above my head, and the canopy spun around. But I was too late, and I drifted well beyond the drop zone, over a barbed wire fence and into a manured field about four hundred yards from the target.

As the ground rushed up to meet me, I remembered to lock my feet together to prepare for the PLF and to look away so I wouldn't anticipate impact. My boots slammed into the soil with startling force, and my attempt at a PLF failed. I bounced off my feet and onto my ass, and my teeth snapped together like the jaws of a steel trap. It was a rude and jarring spectacle, but I was high, flying on adrenaline. I peeled myself off the ground and leaped up to collapse the billowing canopy before it dragged me off. I whooped and yelped as I danced around the chute, gathering it in folds to my loving bosom.

A gaggle of jumpers bounced over in a pickup, all smiles and congratulations. New jumpers bought the beer, they shouted. You bet! Line 'em up!

That rite was over; a passage had been made. Had I gained anything from my self-imposed test of manhood? Had the jump been something more than one hell of a thrill? Over a meritorious, contemplative beer, I decided it was. I had earned the confidence that comes from consciously overcoming terror. I could know that, at least once, I had decisively mastered fear—had willingly flouted danger. I wouldn't have to spend the rest of my life proving myself, enduring endless internal debates about courage, control, and worthiness. It had been a true passage in that I wouldn't have to pass that way again. I *could* (and would), but I didn't *need* to. The next time would be for pleasure rather than proof. A burden was lifted from my shoulders; my own mind was satisfied, and that's the toughest taskmaster.

I wrote a story about our jumps for the college paper, and we weren't accused of sin—only madness. But another activity frowned upon by the administration was hitch-hiking; it wasn't at all Ambassador-like. That's one reason why Wayne Janes and I set off across Texas with our thumbs.

"I acknowledge the Furies . . . I have heard
the disastrous beating of their wings."

Theodore Dreiser

Mark Coyle

Bumming with the Furies

We stood on the shoulder of the interstate for five hours. The skyscrapers of Houston loomed over us in the hazy south Texas sky, and I grew to loathe them. Their haughty immensity mocked our faded jeans, worn boots, and soiled field jackets. A thousand cars passed by, ignoring our thumbs.

Wayne and I discussed the tactic of sticking a five dollar bill between my fingers—not as a lure for the greedy, but as a demonstration of our desperation. Finally we decided that before sinking that low it would be better to fry our brains on the sun-baked pavement. It was a matter of principle.

"Principle?" grated the Furies. "So it's another matter of principle is it?" Their ethereal, discarnate voices dripped with sarcasm and malice—or so I imagined—because it seems we always pay for our principles, and the pattern held true in sweltering Houston. A vehicle eventually stopped. It was a battered Ford pickup with a smiling family of five crammed into the cab. The father apologetically hooked a thumb toward the truck box and shrugged as if to say, "Sorry, boys; take it or leave it." The box was level-full of household garbage. Wayne and I managed to smile back as we clambered over the sides of the box and nestled into the milk cartons, coffee grounds, and soggy paper towels. As the truck pulled into traffic, was that laughter I heard, a devilish cackling from the hot sky?

Still, the garbage was soft, and, as we cruised through the center of bustling, opulent Houston, we fancied ourselves as comfortable as the staring oil barons who whisked by in their air-conditioned Cadillacs and Lincolns. (No doubt, though, they smelled better.) But this wasn't the strangest ride on our pilgrimage to the Gulf of Mexico, on our winsome journey to the sea.

We were restless, under a puissant spell with a melodious name: wanderlust. There was no practical reason for hitch-hiking to the Gulf. I had a long-lost friend in Corpus Christi, but that was only a pretext. (As it turned out, we never even made it to Corpus.) The lust for the Road was irresistible. The prospects for adventure, danger, and romance seemed excellent. We were free to wander where we wished. Besides, I had never seen the ocean. If we hadn't been en-rolled in a fundamentalist Bible college and restrained by notions of responsibility and obligation (0, cruel upbringing!), we would have preferred to ship out on some tramp steamer, swabbing decks and chipping paint in exchange for a chance at contracting exotic diseases. Instead we would thumb to the coast, easily seduced by the apparent freedom of the open highway. It seemed we had everything to gain.

Wayne and I were both theology majors—sporting IV-D draft deferments and aiming for the ministry—and our weak imitation of *Easy Rider* (sans "hogs") was an act of rebellion. Our journey, had we not kept it secret, would have been strongly discouraged. Bum-ming the highways in an earthly escapade of *joi de vivre* was not ap-proved fundamentalist behavior. That added a sense of delicious disobedience to our trek. Actually, the administration was missing the boat. They should have expressly dispatched all ministerial candidates out on the road for a couple of months—with almost no cash—to savor the grit of the world and put an edge on their faith. It could have been considered part of the final exams. There's nothing like low-cost, long-distance bumming to bring out true character.

I had hitchhiked enough before college to know that some possess a golden thumb. I knew a guy who hitched from Dallas to Minneapolis in less than twenty hours. I would be hard-pressed to match that by driving myself. I think it was his benign, harmless face—it was puppy-like. Mothers with toddlers would pick him up. Wayne and I didn't enjoy the blessing of cuteness. Our mugs weren't exactly menacing, though they weren't Cocoa Puffs box material either. But since Corpus Christi was only about 350 miles away, we figured we could get there and back in two or three days, depending on the vicissitudes of the road and, of course, the Furies. They had it in for us from the start.

We had to *walk* the first eleven miles, at night, in a hammering East Texas downpour. (Toad-stranglers, they call them.) In the dark puddles I could see the canine head of Tisiphone, leering remorselessly. What was our crime? The hubris of seeking freedom? The cars splashed us as they sped by, unheeding.

Finally a driver stopped, but it wasn't for free. He was piloting a tractor/trailer rig, a double-decker cattle bus packed with bawling Herefords headed for doomsday. His eyes were like theirs—wide open and glazed. He boasted he had driven 8,000 miles in the last six days. He was popping pills and riding the ragged edge of disaster. He made us an offer: if we'd help him unload the cattle at the stockyards in Henderson, we could ride there with him.

So at around 2:00 a.m. we played cowboys. It seemed an odd hour for such activity, and I wondered in passing if we were handling contraband. I could just picture some enraged rancher, puffing on Marlboros and cursing commie/hippie/rustlers as he lynched us from the nearest white oak tree. Deep in my brain the malicious Furies harmonized on a mocking chorus of "Hang Down Your Head, Tom Dooley."

Wayne and I had the easy job. We perched on the sides of the chute that led down to the corral and slapped bovine butts to keep them humping as they exited the trailer. The cattle were not enamored of that chute, and we had to rudely hustle them along. It was almost fun. "Git along little, doggies!" I yelled, wishing I had a coiled lariat.

Our host, meanwhile, was *inside* the trailer doing the same. Anyone who has been around cattle, especially frightened cattle, knows how insane that is. The driver was unperturbed. "There's only one real bad one," he informed us, "and he'll come out last."

Sure enough, in about a half hour all that was left in the trailer was a stubborn, onery bull holed up at the far end of the top deck. Our driver assured us: "This one'll be a bastard." Grasping an electric cattle prod in each hand, he strode into the dark trailer, heading for the proverbial showdown. There ensued an awful, zany racket, like something off a cartoon soundtrack. The bull bellowed in anger, bashing against the sides of the trailer. The driver loudly and fluently cursed as the prods zapped and crackled. The wild clash went on for long minutes, and to my mind the outcome was in doubt. But finally the unhappy bull stampeded to the head of the chute, our champion hot on its tail to administer a final boot as it rumbled down to the corral.

The man turned to us, his zombie eyes aflame with the thrill of the joust. He grinned crookedly and said, "I told you that one would be a bastard!" Ah, the romance of the open road. As per our agreement, he drove us to the edge of town, and Wayne and I resumed hiking.

The rain had stopped, but at that hour so had the traffic. We walked for a couple of miles and then sat on the shoulder to rest. Soon we saw the glow of headlights coming around a bend. It was another semi, and we were hopeful. Little did we know that hideous Megaera perched atop the cab, beating her bat-like wings. For as the truck roared past, white feathery creatures flew out the back, like fluttering, tattered ghosts. A flapping body fell in front of us, then another, and further down the road yet one more. We flinched and ducked. For a moment we didn't understand what was happening. Were we being assaulted? But then we saw the receding truck was piled high with poultry cages, and it was leaving a trail of chicken corpses in its wake. It was a macabre and gruesome vision, a post-midnight portent. Pelted with weird fowls dredged from some nightmare, I was momentarily spooked. Images flashed through my mind—tabloid headlines: death on the highway, serial killers, expendable lives, ritual murder—all tied-in with hitchhiking. I wondered if the luckless chickens were dead before they left the truck, and if so, how that would affect the quality of the canned soup that was more than likely their destiny? It was hilarious in a twisted sort of way—an incriminating trail of chickens. Did Colonel Sanders know about this?

Soon after, we got a short ride into Mount Enterprise, little more than a wide spot in the road. We took a leisurely, two-minute stroll across town, and were just on the outskirts when a squad car pulled up alongside us. It was 4:00 a.m. The officer behind the wheel, modeled after the Hollywood stereotype of Southern lawmen, was a fat, mean-looking, "good ol' boy." His cowboy hat sported a large shiny badge. He looked like he chewed Redman. He rolled down his window and favored us with a hostile, searching glare.

"Wutch y'all doin', boys?" he asked. His inflection was that policemen's perfect blend of polite inquiry and veiled threat.

"We're just walking out of town," I replied.

"Well, that's real good, son. Y'all just keep on a-walkin'."

"Yes sir."

The man knew troublemakers when he saw them. We, on the other hand, knew trouble when we saw it. There was no room here for harmless ministerial students, and we didn't tarry to see what enterprise had been mounted in that locality. We couldn't hear freedom ringing.

We moved south in little jumps. Everyone who picked us up seemed to be going "just a few miles down the road a ways." At one point we got a lift from a burly white man who purported to be an ex-Marine. He immediately launched into a series of grisly stories and was entertaining himself so thoroughly that when we reached the town where he had originally intended to drop us, he decided to go on to the next. He did this twice. Apparently he wasn't blessed with a captive audience very often. One of his tales concerned the foul night he and his buddy Zack had supposedly "torched a nigger." They tied him up inside his own house and then set it afire. I was disturbed to think that Wayne and I may have appeared like the kind of folks who would enjoy hearing obnoxious racist stories. (I suppose being white was enough.) The man was lying, but it was frightening to see how much relish there was in the telling. In any case, we were such stimulating company—we never got a word in edgewise—that he finally said, "Hell. If I had a six-pack I believe I'd drive you boys all the way to the coast!" Nevertheless, his stories petered out, and he pulled over. We didn't offer to buy any beer; we had been captive long enough.

The wicked Furies turned playful. As fate would have it, our very next ride was a black man in a white Caddy—cross my heart and hope to die. His hot pink shirt dazzled our pavement-seared eyes. Peering from beneath the wide brim of a felt hat festooned with feathers, he said, "A little somethin' fo' yo' head, man?"—and offered us a joint. We declined, but it was obvious he had been making liberal use of the weed himself; his head was in fine shape. He wound that Cadillac up to nearly 100 miles per hour and then slouched lazily back in the seat. I prayed his motor skills were up to the task of holding that speeding bomb to the road. Leering Alecto, her evil head sprouting snakes instead of hair, was dancing lasciviously on the hood, or at least in my fidgeting mind. But, foot to the floor and roach to the lips, the black man got us safely, if not securely, into Houston. He told us white boys no grisly stories.

In Houston, as I said, we lounged in garbage while touring the city. Our slow progress had put Corpus Christi out of reach. Pity. I would've liked to have seen the city that shares its name with both the Messiah and a U.S. Navy nuclear attack submarine. Is there, I wonder, some little town in the Midwest named Armageddon (in Ohio, perhaps), for which a sister ship could be named? Our national sense of humor (you'll recall we elected a movie cowboy to the presidency) would be well served.

In lieu of Corpus, we flagged a ride to Freeport, on the Gulf Coast just south of Houston. The driver, a friendly guy about our own age, served us some Colt 45 malt liquor and escorted us on a tour of his mobile home. He offered to put us up for the night, but we politely demurred, preferring the manly rigors of roadside ditches to the decadent luxury of warm, dry beds. After all, when would we have the opportunity to do something like this again? In a few years, as it turned out, Wayne would be a chemical engineer for Exxon; he would also be a husband and father. When worked into those kinds of situations, one doesn't get to sleep in ditches anymore.

After the trailerhome tour, the guy drove us right onto the

beach. So, there was the sea. We drank a Coke, waded in the surf for a few minutes, then left. Destinations are a drag. It's being on the road that counts.

By nightfall we were back on a Houston freeway, thumbs in the breeze. To our surprise we got a ride almost instantly, and I foolishly thought the vindictive Furies had curbed their wrath. But alas, they'd only grown more cruelly clever, for the bearded, unkempt driver with the greasy ponytail was obviously possessed.

He was driving a van, a model with the engine compartment between the front seats. But this vehicle had been customized. The passenger seat had been removed to make room for a larger engine. It lay there fully exposed in all its mechanical glory, crowding the passenger space. It seemed a minor inconvenience at first, and I thought nothing of it as Wayne climbed into the back of the van and I squatted where the front seat should have been. The etiquette of the road demanded that one of us keep our host company up front. I quickly realized, however, that my courteous gesture was both irrelevant and dangerous.

As soon as I closed the door, the madman punched the gas pedal to the firewall and we blasted off. The engine was screaming only inches from my thigh, and I could feel heat on my flesh. The whirling fan blades looked like a buzzsaw, a deadly blur of pitiless metal. The van kept accelerating until the speedometer read a horrifying 130 miles per hour. The driver gripped the wheel tightly in both hands, grinning out the windshield, grinning at the engine, grinning at me. He shouted something above the roar, but I couldn't make it out. If I had replied, I would have said something insulting and obscene. I kept slipping toward the hot motor and menacing fan. I groped for the door handle to steady myself and found it was missing. I desperately dug my fingernails into the strip of felt between the window and the door metal, hanging on by the slimmest of purchases, understanding that one good bump and that engine would transform significant portions of my body into chopped, cooked meat. In the back, Wayne was gagging on exhaust fumes and waste heat. The engine thundered and Tisiphone howled, a rabid bitch baying at the moon. Her sisters shrieked and whined like a 130 miles per hour wind. No doubt they gnawed at the tires. I could envision us as a smear on the highway—grotesquely lit by flashing red lights.

Mercifully, our host could only take us ten miles. The ride lasted about five minutes. "Sorry I can't take you farther," he grinned. Not to worry, that was quite all right. My fingers were already cramped, and my eyes were watering from fumes and the power of pure velocity.

As we had the day before, we proceeded in short hops, and around midnight we were camped on the interstate outside of Huntsville, home of the Texas state prison. After more than thirty hours of traveling, we were exhausted. We lay down just off the shoulder of an exit ramp and fell asleep. Sometime after 2:00 a.m. we were awakened, blinded by the glare of headlights. Squinting in the brightness, we could see two silhouetted forms silently approaching. We leaped to our feet, imaginations amok concerning the nocturnal possibilities of being near a major prison.

When we rose, the dark forms halted, and one of them said, "Oh. I thought you guys were dead." And they walked off. Their nonchalant manner made me wonder about the frequency of finding corpses lying around near Huntsville. As they drove away, we saw they were in a garbage truck. Strange. The Furies continued to associate us with trash.

And we certainly felt like it—worn, dirty, unwanted. We started trudging down the grassy median of Interstate 45 and humped it for a long time. Toward dawn a truckdriver pulled over. He made it clear the only reason he was picking us up was because he was tired and bored and required some conversation. We did our best to oblige, but fatigue won out. The man was saying something profound about archery when I nodded off, my head bouncing senselessly against the window. I don't think the driver noticed. Wayne, sitting next to him, made a more valiant effort, but when he fell asleep with his head on the trucker's shoulder, that tore it.

In my next moment of awareness we were parked at a truck stop, and the driver was roughly shaking us awake. He was angry. He hustled us into the restaurant and pumped us full of coffee. He warned that if caffeine didn't work we'd be hiking again very soon.

Back on the road, we paid close attention as the trucker lectured us about the hazards of the highway. He demonstrated the correct way to hold a steering wheel, cautioning us to never hook our thumbs around the spokes. Both of his thumbs were broken once when he had had a blowout and the wheel was violently jerked around in his hands. He was also emphatic about what *not* to hit: "Hit a horse, hit a light pole, hit a deer, but never *ever* hit a pig—like a damn brick wall!" To this day I never hook my thumbs around a steering wheel, and I dread the thought of encountering a hog on the highway. Will I have the presence of mind to "just hit the ditch?" The driver assured us it would be the wiser course.

As the sun rose and revealed a fresh, glistening April morning, he let us off on a single-lane road near Corsicana, and we resumed hiking and thumbing. Less than ten minutes later we had our second encounter with the law. A local cop passed us, then spun around and raced back. He stepped out of the car and confronted us.

"Hitchhiking," he said, "is illegal in Texas. Don't you boys know enough *not* to stick out your thumbs when you see a cop coming?"

He asked us how the weather was on the coast, then left. I guess it was too early in the morning to be *officially* messing with the likes of us.

That minor failure of the law enforcement system was apparently too much for the Furies. They vaporized in brilliant sunshine. Though her cold, reptilian hair craved heat, even Alecto faded away into the ephemeral, encephalous mist of my neurons.

I understood then the mythical freedom of hitchhiking. Mythical, because there is no freedom. You can only go where the road goes. You can only go as fast and as far as those who pick you up. We were prisoners of time, chance, and asphalt. Nevertheless, the morning infused us with renewed vigor and lofty spirits. The last delicate tendrils of pre-dawn fog lingered in the ditches. The grass and trees were verdant—their springtime greens enriched by the saturating rays of the rising sun. The cool air was tangy with the aroma of wild flowers and dew. The highway stretched before us, like the beckoning smile of a temptress leading us astray. It felt good to breathe. It was comforting to walk. And to grin.

Wayne tersely summed up the trip in his journal: "On the road 39 hours, thumbed 2,405 cars, got 30 rides. Longest was from Huntsville to Corsicana [114 miles]. Shortest was some gal who picked us up and then dropped us off before I could sit down. Traveled 640 miles. Was up 56 hours running and flunked a German test the next day."

It's sometimes a glorious thing to be on the road. Just don't ever mistake it for freedom.

*". . . let us run with patience
the race that is set before us."*

Hebrews 12:1

Mark Coyle

The Seven Golden Cheetahs

There *was* a road, however, that offered us a brand of freedom that had nothing to do with going anywhere. In fact, this road was most often a great loop that ended where it began. It was a marathon course, and once initiated into the demanding cult of long-distance running, it was as tough to quit as a drug habit. Some of us discovered that the more we disciplined our bodies, the more our minds were released to the nether regions of biochemical mystery—where stress evaporated, and insights into the human condition sometimes arrived with the sudden impact of a thunderclap. I trained like an animal and ran four marathons in two years. An image from my last race is etched into memory.

Feeney was vomiting as he ran. His splattered, beaten legs, rubbery after twenty-six miles, seemed to be moving in slow motion. The last hundred yards were ghastly—each broken stride an exercise in agony. His face was a twisted caricature of the human visage we had known some four hours before. We were tempted to run out, grab him and scream for first aid, but we resisted the criminal impulse. Feeney didn't want mercy, he just wanted to finish. We had no right to rob him of his suffering. (A marathon isn't merely a race—

it's a trial—a path to enlightenment and justification. There are to be no mediators between man and marathon.) His T-shirt fouled with black puke, Feeney raised his hands at the finish line and collapsed into our arms. His legs quit—temporarily destroyed. We carried him from the middle of the street and laid him in the gutter. If someone had felt for a pulse and said, "My God, he's dead!" I wouldn't have been surprised. But Feeney lived, passing only into legend.

Just down the avenue, bisecting the hazy sky, was the shining span of St. Louis' Gateway Arch. It would've made a great wide-angle photo: in the foreground lies Feeney, sprawled on the pavement, the color of a cadaver; behind him rise the dark lines of the cityscape with the triumphal Arch dominating the background. If I had such a photo, perhaps I could just point to it and say, "Yeah, that's what it's all about—there's the glory of marathons." But the graphic image doesn't exist, and I suppose it would've been too abstract. From the picture alone, one might have concluded that Feeney was the victim of a brutal mugging or had just been sideswiped by a truck.

Instead I could display my "Marathon Log Book," a personal record of training that we all kept at the behest of our running coach. I could recite hard data. For instance, on one mild day in springtime I ran a fifteen-miler. My weight before the run was 192, afterwards 186. Or I could plot my resting pulse rate from sixty-six beats per minute at the start of training down to near thirty a couple months later. After the marathon in St. Louis, my pulse rate was still at 106 beats per minute an hour after the race. I usually logged about fifty miles per week.

In conjunction with such stats, I could describe the euphoria out on the fifteen-mile training course. Cruising in high gear, loping along at six-and-a-half minutes per mile, my partner would suddenly emit an exuberant whoop. He would dance a little stutter step and shout, "I can fly! I can fly!"—laughing at the clouds. The road seemed to wind into the sky, and we could run forever. "No pain!" I would yell back, "No pain!" And there wasn't. It took a lot of miles to get there, and it was worth every step. It was a natural, heart-pounding, brain-goosing rush.

But talking about being high is like trying to accurately convey how something tastes or smells—everything is lost in translation. Maybe the best way to tell of the lure and addiction of marathons and distance running is to share our group's florid, communal fantasy. It went like this:

"I can see 'em! I can see 'em, Coach—The Seven Golden Cheetahs!"

The Janes Boy screamed this toward the end of our ninth, guts-out 440. I hadn't glimpsed them myself, I had yet to attain righteousness. After a sixty-second rest, Coach's wicked whistle ordered us out for another lap, and that one did it. On the final turn, pumping for the finish, lungs flat-out-to-the-max, I reached that painless plateau of Runner's Nirvana.

Coach was beaming, the grin a bit twisted. He knew a good workout when he saw one. Employing that shrill, merciless whistle and selected sarcastic taunts, he had driven us into another vision of paradise. We were feeling no pain and bearing no grudge. This is why we ran—it felt so good to stop, to waft into a supine position and meditate upon the transcendental nature of utter inactivity. How liberating to pay up your oxygen debt.

But ironically, the first revelation of Runner's Nirvana had come to light in the locker room. We were just slouching around after a brisk ten-mile run, sweating and breathing (how fine!), when someone wondered aloud about Dugger. Whatever had become of Dugger, our champion marathon man? No one had seen the maniac lately. Then one of the better runners, a gaunt and wirey specimen called Dead Bones, got a faraway look in his bloodshot eyes and somberly unveiled the Mystery.

Dugger had been running a marathon, Dead Bones explained. It was a fast, inspired race. At the twenty-two-mile mark he was maintaining a god-like pace of 4:45 per mile. That would put him at the finish with a time under 2:05:00, a quantum leap better than the world record—and that on a hilly, windy, ugly course. But as Dugger approached mile twenty-three, he grew faint. Spectators could see him fading. His red shorts were turning pink, his black hair gray. He was becoming difficult to see as he jacked up his incredible pace even further. Soon his body was translucent, his feet an ephemeral blur. Just past twenty-three miles he vanished—accelerating into thin air. One witness heard a distant, exultant cry of, "I can see 'em, Coach! I can see 'em!" Then nothing.

Dead Bones paused and, before continuing, pulled a jockstrap over his head. He was trembling with reverence, said he needed extra support. The Janes Boy was transfixed, a Gatorade growing warm in his hand. He'd been in the same race, trailing Dugger by two miles. After the start, he had never seen him again. Dugger had blasted off like he was running a stinking 220. Still, the Janes Boy could have sworn Dugger had black shorts and red hair. Strange. But then the Janes Boy's idea of carbohydrate loading was downing a six-pack of Budweiser. In short, he was ripe for the revelation.

Dead Bones solemnly surveyed our expectant faces through a leg hole of the jock. He appeared to be debating our worthiness. But then the Janes Boy baptized him with the Gatorade, and Dead Bones' tongue was loosened.

Dugger, he said, had passed into Runner's Nirvana. And we could too, if we suffered enough. There was more to life than a low resting pulse rate, and here was what awaited the deserving: as you fade from the track, your frenetic pace becomes effortless. Your blood is saturated with oxygen, your brain gorged with endorphins. It's scary at first—pleasant and good, and therefore weird. Then there they are—The Seven Golden Cheetahs. They're just ahead, loping in long graceful strides at about sixty miles per hour. Incredibly, despite the lousy aerodynamics of being human, you gain on them, feeling more like a Porsche than a person. The Cheetahs lead you over a rise and then evaporate in a burst of speed. You stop and gaze on your reward.

Below, there is a limpid, greenish-yellow pool about 440 yards across. You walk down, cup your hands and take a sip. Ah, sweet electrolytes! As you guzzle your fill, a melodious tune drifts over the surface of the pool. It's the sound of a whistle being blown very softly. You look up and on the other side of the pool is Coach. He's sitting cross-legged, peaceful and at rest. Languidly, he beckons you and tosses his whistle into the pool. It disappears forever. You wade over and gratefully buss each pure golden eyelet of his satin New Balance running shoes. A trio of Amazons materialize (Women's Runners' Nirvana is just over the next hill) to smear Atomic Balm over your entire body. As your resting pulse rate reaches a new low and the Amazons bend over you, Coach can hear you whisper, "I see 'em. I can see 'em."

Then someone snapped the elastic band on the jockstrap, and Dead Bones was dumped back into reality. "Infidels!" he shrieked from the floor. But he was wrong; we believed him. There had to be something to ease our earthly anguish—and the Budweiser wasn't cutting it.

So we ran . . . and ran and ran and ran. And every now and then one of us would disappear, following Dugger into oblivion. (Actually, he was in California—but close enough.) Soon we were all gone, retired from the agony. Coach is gone too. The last I heard he was erecting pole barns in North Dakota. It seems a harsh sentence, but that whistle was mean.

"Look for a tough wedge for a tough log."

Publius

Patrick Dwyer

The Foreign Legion Syndrome

In the summer of 1973, before my final year at AC, I contracted a case of what we called the Foreign Legion Syndrome. It was an overwhelming youthful restlessness, a sublime yearning that consumed caution and responsibility in a juvenescent flame. It was desire for change, lust for experience. It was forward motion—flat-out, and don't look back. But it was also a retreat, withdrawal from the status quo. Whether it was a romantic entanglement grown too complex, a financial predicament too tiresome to face, or an identity crisis too painful to identify, part of the Syndrome was *escape*.

The idea was to run away, far away, and do something interesting when you arrived. The Syndrome seemed to strike at age seventeen or eighteen and taper off in the mid-twenties, though in some cases it has been known to be chronic and/or terminal. Many victims ended up in the military, perhaps a few in the real Foreign Legion. But there are other paths to follow just as therapeutic.

I chose a logging crew in the Oregon Cascades. There were several advantages: it was far from home, it was hard and dangerous, it was alien to my previous experience, and it was damn good money. Perhaps to say "I chose" is deceptive—it implies contemplation. Like all true Syndrome cases, going there was a spur-of-the-moment decision made after midnight in response to a chance opportunity, as when people express their arguments in favor of such a decision with convincing, introspective expressions such as: "Go for it!"

I arrived in Oregon on a Sunday afternoon and went to work on Monday morning. The owner of the small logging company—who was also the foreman, or "Hook," out in the woods—delivered a short, but captivating orientation spiel. It was chiefly about safety, or rather the lack of it. He closed by saying, "Be careful! I can't afford to bury you." As if his financial affairs would be of concern to my corpse. But brimming with naivete, I actually believed the man was worried about us. Fortunately, in the throes of the Syndrome, *education* is always near.

One morning, after a long week of apprenticeship on the brush-stacking crew—a grueling, miserable, mind-numbing ordeal—I was given the job of "chaser." My predecessor in the position, a seasoned professional logger, had just had a short but heated tête-á-tête with the Hook, and had "resigned." I was the first warm body the Hook laid eyes on, and I was conscripted as a replacement. Seniority and other trappings of unionism were not popular in the woods.

The title "chaser" was the job description. I chased from one duty to the next—from log branding, to limbing, to truck hookups, to greasing equipment. But the primary duty was on the landing, releasing the cable slings, or "chokers," from around the logs as they were dragged out of the forest by the "yarder."

A yarder is a gargantuan, crane-like machine with a massive boom. From a pulley at the top of the boom, we strung up to three-quarters of a mile of hefty steel cable down the mountainside through the woods. We mounted another pulley on the biggest tree we could find, then wound the cable around it and returned it to the yarder. This formed an awesome steel "clothesline" along which a hoist was driven. The hoist, about the size of a Volkswagen Bug, traveled along the clothesline and could drop up to four chokers, like menacing tentacles, down to the forest floor. These chokers—they work like they sound—were looped around felled trees. We were dealing with Douglas fir logs, anywhere from two to six feet in diameter and cut into thirty-five-foot "sticks." This was no spruce-bog pulp operation; we're talking big-league timber.

The yarder and hoist would "walk" these titanic logs up the mountainside and deposit them in a pile on the landing. The chaser's task was to unhook the chokers. It didn't take an engineer to figure it out, but there were a few variables that added a certain deadly playfulness to the operation. The pile, which sometimes grew to be fifteen or twenty feet high, was often unstable, and it was easy for me to picture the consequences of having a three-ton log roll over my body. But the pile/trap wasn't the worst of it. While the yarder was stacking logs on the landing, they were being simultaneously loaded onto trucks. The loader was a tracked vehicle, similar to an old steam cable shovel, but in place of the bucket was a large set of toothed jaws. They looked and worked like the pincers of a monstrous crab. The loader was parked next to the yarder, and with methodical swiftness the loader operator swiveled his machine from the pile to a waiting truck. It was a wondrous brand of efficient, mechanical brutality. Huge logs were slung through the air, steel jaws biting into bark, steel cables whining (and sometimes snapping) under the strain of violent jerks—all of it dominated by the relentless roar of large diesel engines.

As chaser, my forays to the log pile had to be timed with precision. Judging how long it would take to unhook the chokers and estimating how soon the loader would swing back for another log, I had to decide if it was safe to leap upon the pile or wait for another pass. I also kept in mind that time was money, and my job was to be done as quickly as possible. Relying upon experience (of which I had none at the start), I had to balance personal safety with maximum production. A few of the variables were obvious: bigger logs took longer to load and vice versa, and it was harder to unhook chokers that were pinched between logs. But one of the wild cards in the deck was that the loader operator had a restricted field of view and often didn't know if I was on the pile or not. I'd been pointedly informed that I had sole responsibility "for your own ass."

One afternoon, due to mechanical troubles with the loader, the pile was expanding well beyond the stage of efficient handling. To expedite matters, the loader operator became selective about what he put on the trucks. When he yanked a smaller log out of the pile, he might just swing it out of the way and drop it, bitching about "pecker poles" and returning the jaws to the pile as swiftly as possible. I had no foolproof method of determining which logs he was going to load and which he was going to cast aside. This upped the ante considerably. At one point, he grabbed what looked to me like a keeper, and I assumed he would load it. I grabbed the opportunity to scramble up the pile to catch up on my branding. (This consisted of a hard blow to the ends of the logs with a branding axe, the head of which left our distinctive mark and number for future reference at the mill.) I figured I had about a minute, and I could do a lot of branding in sixty seconds.

I was hard at it when something caused me to stop short. As near as I could remember later, it was a sound that gave away the danger—a grinding of gears, a low whistle of wind past metal—I couldn't be sure, but I jerked my head up in time to see nothing but the clenched steel jaws, bark impaled on their teeth, headed right for my face. I sprang from the ten-foot pile and hit the ground running. The jaws ripped directly over my former perch, grazing the log on which I'd been standing. As if bewitched by some demonic power, they completed their wide arc and swung off the pile after me. As I sprinted toward the yarder I could see its operator staring, his face frozen in horror. "It wasn't that bad," I thought, but fortunately I wasn't seeing what he was. The jaws were directly behind me and closing rapidly. At that moment, the loader operator swiveled to the point where he could see me and, thinking quickly, he opened the jaws—they sailed by, bracketing my body. I had passed, so to speak, through the jaws of death. All I saw was their shadow on the ground, like a swooping bird of prey. I felt a rush of air as they whipped by.

I slumped against the track of the yarder, breathless. And upset. I figured the Hook, who also happened to be the loader operator, was going to be angry because I had almost been killed. He was a stickler for safety, remember? But when he jumped out of the cab I was shocked to see he was laughing uproariously. He strode over and slapped my back, bellowing, "Well, I guess that'll put the fear of God into you!" Yeah. Safety first. But then a case of the Syndrome did not curry the favor of fate.

Two days later while I was preparing to hook up a truck (the long tandem rigs came up the mountain carrying their eight rear wheels piggyback, and we plucked them off with our loader and re-attached them), a steel cable snapped in the middle of the procedure, and the eight big wheels fell ten feet and crashed to the ground less than twelve inches from the toes of my boots. The Hook and I exchanged glances, and he shook his head and shrugged. If there was a stressed steel cable with my name on it, there wasn't much he could do about it. I remember thinking that if this kept up, it was going to be either a very long—or a very short—summer.

There were more close calls. I was issued a brand-new aluminum hard hat on the first day, and after ten weeks it was dented and gouged in a half-dozen places. One windy day the "widow-makers"—limbs and snags—showered like evil rain. But the harrowing moments were not the most trying; it was the everyday occurence—like morning.

I can close my eyes and still relish the images in vivid detail: it's pre-dawn and half-dark as the crew stumbles out of the four-door pickup truck known as a "crummy." Crummy. You said it. A smudge of orange light on the eastern horizon promises another scorching day. I blink and yawn, and the usual case of butterflies seesaws through my gut. Logging still scares the hell out of me at 6:00 a.m. I sit in the doorway of the truck and lace up my stiff, spiked boots. They're an orthopedic nightmare, like they've already been bronzed for the Logging Hall of Fame. The crew moves about in gloomy silence as they psyche themselves up for another shift, sipping one last dose of coffee or priming up on Copenhagen snuff. Suddenly, Russ, our psychopathic assistant foreman, breaks into a raucous, obscene song and leaps to his feet. "Let's go to work!" he yells, and bangs his heavy coffee mug on the helmets of Bob and Greg. "It's a fucking beautiful damn day! Let's go!" As usual, his adjectives are explicit, but incongruent, and seem entirely fitting.

"Russ!" hollers Scotty, our catskinner, "You know what you are Russ? You're a 14-carat, diamond-studded, gold-plated prick!"

Russ merely laughs, a demented, sniggering sound. As we reluctantly heft our gear, the Hook drives up with two new recruits. This happens often; the attrition rate is phenomenal. These two unfortunates are destined for the brush-stacking crew, and I feel the guilty, sadistic glee of one who's already done his time. That hot, hard, and monotonous chain-gang of a detail will suck out their spirits in two days. The Hook introduces them, but the odds are they won't last a week, so I pay little attention to names. As we start trudging down the dusty road toward the landing, the snow-capped peak of Mount Theilsen glowing yellow-orange in the distance, Russ makes another pass with his mug, catching me on the brim of my hard hat and shoving it down over my eyes. I utter the customary curses, but I also grin as I realize I'm almost beginning to like the miserable scumbag. Scotty climbs onto his D-4 Cat, and it won't start. He begins to holler again: "Why you monkey-wards, treasure-city, payless piece of shit!" The man's a poet. Bob's chainsaw coughs, smokes and roars. Another day.

And they seemed endless; ten-hour days with fifteen minutes for lunch, the steady work broken up only by mechanical breakdowns or stolen moments on the run—moments when the philosophy of these hard-core loggers briefly surfaced amid the din and rush of hustling machines.

One day, for instance, Scotty and I were dragging lengths of steel cable and a gang of iron fittings up a steep, brush-entangled mountainside. We took a short break, both of us momentarily spent— he because of age, I due to the altitude. With sweat beaded on his forehead and his chest heaving slightly in the thin air, the old logger leaned on a stump. His eyes glinted, and he flashed me a sagacious grin as he said: "You know, you got to be in the woods a long time to get as crazy as I am. You got to *lean* into it. If you go crazy overnight, they'll take you away."

We both laughed and resumed our work, but he'd struck a chord. In those few words were distilled the essence of that summer in the Cascades. I had fled to the mountains to keep from "leaning." The Foreign Legion Syndrome was an attempt at sanity, at the maintenance of a healthy mind. I had jumped a rut to form a new track.

When my mind tried to close again, lulled to sleepiness by the routine of staying alive, the door would be just a little more stubborn. We must keep on being surprised. For example, just when I thought I knew everything there was to know about Douglas fir logs, Russ found one full of bees. Employing a talent for wicked pranks, he deftly slipped a choker around it and sent it up to me on the landing. Amazingly, the hive outlasted the rough ride, and when I leaped aboard to loosen the choker, I was stung five times on the back of the neck before I knew what was happening. I did a wild, impromptu jig on top of the pile and then tore out of there, said Russ, "like a stripe-assed ape." Russ nearly died, convulsed and prostrate in his mirth. I kept an open mind about logs after that.

With what little free time and energy I had, I often walked the streets of Roseburg, "The Logging Capital of the World," where "happiness is a three-log load." It was a facet of the Syndrome that forced one to spend a great deal of time in contemplation, and Roseburg was conducive to that. Never, outside a hospital, have I seen so many maimed and crippled bodies—logging injuries. Wheelchairs and crutches were part of the natural ambience. For a neophyte logger, it was thought-provoking.

One evening in early August, as I was strolling on a road above the Umpqua River, I was approached by two young women. Russ would've called them "hippie types." They pulled alongside in a Volkswagen Beetle complete with peace sign sticker, and one of them leaned out the window.

"Hey," she said, "you want to go with us and chant for world peace?"

I thought about it for a moment and declined. I was polite, but firm, and they drove off. Yes, ladies, I thought, run off to your own Foreign Legion. Look me up again in a few years; I bet you won't be chanting anymore. I sure as hell won't be logging.

"But after all it's what we've done
that makes us what we are."

Jim Croce

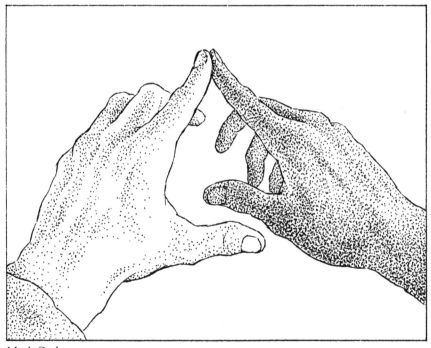

Mark Coyle

Different Blood

The logging, the skydiving, the marathons—all were rites of passage and seem more important as years accumulate. But the people we know are as critical as the deeds we do, and few things will shape experience as profoundly as a good friend (or a good enemy).

In the late teens and early twenties, the theory and practice of friendship is made more complicated by matters of gender. Ambassador College sought to streamline relations between the sexes by marshalling us into a puritanical lifestyle patterned on Old Testament strictures.

Adhering to a code of behavior featuring rigid sexual rules was no mean feat for post-adolescent (barely) college students. Although it was understood that females were admitted primarily to provide a pool of ministerial wife candidates, "going steady" was prohibited until your senior year, and all but handholding and chaste, fraternal kissing was forbidden until marriage. There were violations, of course, but scant toleration—students were known to be expelled for no more than "heavy-petting." Since this was "God's College," the stakes were high—all the way up to eternal salvation—so enforcement wasn't as great a problem as one might suppose.

The student body included a small representation of blacks (about five percent) and one of the absolute taboos was interracial dating. A few *intra*racial couples had gained clemency for dating/ sexual miscues, but it was clear that an interracial pair would face severe, immediate punishment, with no quarter offered. It was God's will.

I was a true believer and firm supporter of these policies when I met Faye, an attractive black woman who arrived as a student my sophomore year. In retrospect, it's apparent I fell in love with her, though I never admitted it to myself at the time; the consequences of such an emotional state were just too dire.

At our first casual encounters I was intimidated—both by her gender and her race. Being a native of northeastern Minnesota, I hadn't even seen a black person until I was ten years old. I have a vivid memory of watching two black men strolling through our small town neighborhood. My playmates and I were astonished; the only blacks we had ever seen had been on TV and were, there-fore, unreal. We followed the men for three blocks, pointing and whispering—nothing malicious, we were just intensely curious—not unlike African tribesmen encountering their first whites. I assume these men were mere tourists, but for me their appearance was a major event. I had certainly been exposed to the term "nigger" and associated racial slurs, but I had no experience on which to hang genuine prejudice. I had also been assured that all men should be treated equally. And now I could plainly see that these black men were indeed real flesh-and-blood people. Basic, but such are the revelations of a ten-year-old mind.

By the time I was eighteen and actually had met and conversed with a black person, I was nervous about how to behave: how to be inoffensive about not being offensive? How to avoid being unnatural about being natural? How to get past a compulsion to atone for all wrongs my race had done, when I personally had nothing for which to atone? Besides, I had a bashful streak toward people in general, regardless of race, and especially with females.

So in the midst of my ministerial studies, I was suddenly con-fronted with the fact that I was attracted to Faye—not only a black, but most assuredly a female. I was shy, insecure, and brainwashed by a fundamentalist sect. Where did I find the courage to know her?

Partly, it was the racial ban itself. Every white coed was a po-tential mate (and they knew that I knew that they knew), but with Faye that pressure was officially nonexistent. We could be pals and share our time without "dating." By definition we couldn't be romantically involved. We were freed of pretense and awkward courting behavior and could simply be ourselves.

Braver than I, she initiated our friendship. All students were assigned a campus job, and Faye started out in the cafeteria line, dispensing food. One day, as I pushed my tray along the counter at lunchtime, I spilled a glass of milk, and she teased me about it. I spontaneously returned the kidding, and we both laughed. There was chemistry in it, and soon we were walking to classes together and sitting near one another in those we shared, passing irreverent notes spiced with private jokes.

A part of her attraction was this vein of irreverence. She was a faithful member of the flock, but she didn't take the program as seriously as I did. I figured her light-hearted cynicism was the result of being a member of a long-suffering minority (both black and female) forced to take the words and deeds of the establishment with a grain of salt. The flaws and foibles of our instructors (and of the organization itself) were more readily evident to her than to me, and her humor smoothed the edges of implied criticism. Her notes and comments spurred me to thought and reminded me that I'd once been more skeptical myself. Ironically, it was Faye, a descendant of slaves, that subtly (and unwittingly) helped to rekindle a spark of freedom in my mind.

I employed every excuse to spend time with her. Our church was an oppressive, patriarchal outfit that provided separate rules for men and women. For example, a 10:30 p.m. weeknight curfew was imposed on the women, but none was placed on men. So several times a week I'd drive to town "after hours" and return with burgers, tacos, Ripple Wine (her favorite—an ongoing joke), and other goodies for Faye and her dormmates. I had to stop in to collect their money and orders beforehand (and visit) and then make my delivery (and visit) later.

Our friendship soon attracted attention. One afternoon as we were leaving the dining hall together, a white coed announced in passing that we "should be careful." She tried to be jocular about it and failed. The disapproval and hint of scandal were disturbingly clear. I was shocked. I had never thought of Faye as my "girl friend," hadn't dreamed we were engaged in anything illicit. We were two people who liked each other—friends. God, as expounded by our teachers, forbade us to marry, so romance wasn't an option. That's what I told myself—and I half-believed it. Soon after, Faye dropped me a note that quoted Proverbs 18:24: ". . . there is a friend that sticks closer than a brother." Yes, friends. Surely God didn't frown on us for that.

But there were other threats. One evening my friend Bruce tagged along with Faye and me on a trip to a grocery store in town.

(After our warning, we wouldn't have considered going alone.) It had been a hard day for Bruce, and he stretched out in the backseat on the way in. When we arrived at the store he was asleep, and Faye and I decided not to wake him. We knew what he wanted, so we would just buy it. We entered the store together, started shopping in earnest, and I quickly noticed that the proprietor, a middle-aged white male, had me fixed with a malevolent stare. I was puzzled. At the cash register he was brusque to the point of rudeness, literally throwing our items into a bag, and pointedly refraining from a "thank you." We were walking out the door when it hit me. What a naive bumpkin I was! The man had seen Faye and me as a couple—a young man and woman shopping for groceries—probably assumed we were married (or at least living in sin). And like the God of our church, he didn't approve of mixed company. I was mortified; there could've been an ugly, potentially dangerous scene, and I hadn't even thought about it. But upon reflection, I was also pleased. I obviously hadn't considered us as black and white—just me and Faye.

A few weeks later I was accompanying Faye and one of her dormmates across campus. It was after dark, and the rules mandated that women couldn't be out at night without a male escort. You can imagine the inconvenience (not to mention the insult to the women), and everyone hated the policy, but Faye used it as an opportunity. We were strolling along, immersed in three-way chitchat, when she suddenly grabbed my hand and said, "I love you, Peter." I almost choked but quickly replied, "I love you too, Faye." She dropped my hand, and I marveled; it'd been a brilliant move. Marilyn, the other woman, was white, and she and I had been dating enough to be deemed as having "a relationship." With such a significant witness, and considering it was taboo for Faye and me to have a similar "relationship," our mutual declaration of love must then necessarily be Platonic. Marilyn never said a word about it. The episode was innocence itself, and not even I could tell for sure what *kind* of love had been espoused. Did Faye love me "only" as a brother? Did I see her as my "sister?" After agonizing, I finally decided it didn't really matter.

But I also felt compelled to *do* something—to somehow consummate our relationship without sex. Our sect believed that racial difference was epitomized by the blood—not in the actual physical characteristics of hemoglobin, but as a symbol of genetic variation. We were taught that half-breeds were vaguely impure, degenerate in the eyes of God, and that's why the races shouldn't intermarry. Our teachers quoted Leviticus 19:19: "Thou shalt not let thy cattle gender with a diverse kind: thou shalt not sow thy field with mingled seed: neither shall a garment mingled of linen and woollen come upon thee." Though it was conceded via Acts 17 that God had made all men "of one blood," it was emphasized that He had also "determined . . . the bounds of their habitation"—and that didn't include cohabitation. Faye and I discussed this dogma with some skepticism, and it germinated an idea.

I don't remember who suggested it, but we decided we should anoint ourselves "blood brothers." One afternoon, when the lounge of Faye's dorm was deserted, we sat side-by-side on a sofa as I sterilized two needles with a match. Self-consciously giggling, we each pricked our index fingers and squeezed out drops of dark red. Then, suddenly solemn, we slowly pressed our fingers together, rubbing and mixing the blood. I was electrified. It had never been verbalized as a substitute for sex, but to my surprise this special touching was an intensely erotic moment, and the symbolism was overwhelming. Not only were we consummating our emotional ties with an intimate physical act, but we were also rebelling against the notion of different blood and deliberately defying the prejudice of our teachers and society at large. Were we also angering God? We didn't think so. We knew what we were doing; we were "blood brothers," and it was very good.

A year later Faye and I were both happily attached to people of our respective colors, and the four of us had dinner together. It was a pleasant evening, but I've not seen her since. However, I vividly recall our ceremony and how against all odds we transcended race, dogma, and disapproval, cutting our way through the morass to love. It was an educational highlight of my college career, and a well-known Bible verse demonstrated in the flesh. I Corinthians 13:13: "Thus 'faith and hope and love last on, these three,' but the greatest of all is love."

At root it has little to do with religion, a lot to do with some indefinable "chemistry," and nothing to do with blood. But that simple, spontaneous rite amounted to one more step away from the domineering ideology of the Worldwide Church of God.

"... and slime they had for mortar."

Genesis 11:3

Fred Yiran

Rebel of God

The owner of the logging company in Oregon was a Church member, and we regularly attended Sabbath services, but for the first time in almost three years I lived outside the insulating, self-contained, self-centered ambience of the Ambassador College Campus. A friend and I rented an apartment in Roseburg and passed the summer "in the world." The contrast was disturbing.

People on the street weren't toting Bibles and praying about their personal prospects during the Great Tribulation. They didn't recognize my friend and me as called-out servants of the Almighty God. We were just two more faces in the crowd. The nation was abuzz with the Watergate affair (or at least the nation's news media were), and the majority had never heard of the Armstrongs and the WCG and never would. It was humbling to be out of the self-aggrandizing environment of AC. Our natural anonymity reminded me forcefully of something I had read a few months before. At the suggestion of a faculty member whose doubts and questions would soon lead him to resign from AC, I picked up *The Mature Mind*, by H. A. Overstreet. One of the author's key statements was: "A person remains immature, whatever his age, as long as he thinks of himself as an exception to the human race."

It had been drilled into us that we were exceptions, the chosen elite of God. But out in the world at large this was unconvincing. At AC it was easy to forget that we shared the planet with billions of other real human beings, and not just masses of sentient grist for God's judgmental mill—His much-anticipated Day of Wrath. Simple daily exposure to the "unconverted" diluted my elitest outlook.

I was gradually drifting out of the fold, beginning to view the world with my own eyes and not through the filtered lenses of the organization. It wasn't a pleasant sensation. I had turned to the WCG for succor and support—had used the teachings and the tightly-knit infrastructure as a veritable life line. I had completely dedicated my life to the Armstrongs and the Church. I had *believed*, without reservations, for three years. Was I capable of being that mistaken about something so important? Or were my doubts inspired by human weakness and/or the wiles of Satan? I would feel one way in the morning, the opposite by afternoon.

But when I returned to AC in the fall of 1973 (my senior year), I opened the school year with an overt act of rebellion: I officially dropped the fourth-year Bible class and collected a refund of tuition. At a normal school, such an event would have been of little or no consequence, but at AC I was transmitting a clear signal of rejection and disrespect. The class was mandatory for ministerial candidates, and I was therefore removing myself from the "competition" for ordination, the paramount goal of a male AC student. I let it be known that I had dropped the course because, as taught, it was a monumental bore and a waste of time. Since it was being handled by one of the top ten highest-ranking ministers in the WCG, I was hurling an unambiguous insult.

At the time I wasn't sure if I was being brave or apathetic, but I felt giddy, momentarily flushed with the excitement of a free act. I saw it as justified revolt, the vintage wine of human existence. The day I dropped that class I felt more vibrantly alive than I had for a long time. One such act, however trivial it may appear, leads inexorably to another, and I began to aggressively question my teachers. These questions were basically over matters of opinion, and were not earthshaking challenges, but I would never have thought or dared to do it before. The instructors seemed to be caught off guard, unprepared for such resistance, and I went on my way undisciplined and unrebuked. For a time.

That October my whole set of WCG convictions began to quickly unravel. My friend Gerry, a long-time fundamentalist believer who had preached sermons at the age of fifteen (in another denomination) was fighting his way out of religion altogether. He had been researching and discussing doctrine for years, and, coupled with the disillusionment at AC, it was leading him toward atheism. One of the last straws for him at AC was the *Festival Courier* affair.

The *Festival Courier* was a private newspaper/advertising circular Gerry initiated. He designed it for distribution at the Feast of Tabernacles at Big Sandy and hoped to have some fun and make a profit. The Feast was a church convention tailored after the Mosaic festival outlined in the Book of Leviticus. Fifteen thousand or so WCG members annually congregated at the Big Sandy campus in the fall, camping on the spacious grounds for eight days. They attended a daily church service (two on Sabbaths and Holy Days) and spent the "second tithe" money they had saved throughout the year for this specific, commanded purpose. It was a chance for fellowship with other "brethren" from across the nation and for the coveted opportunity to hear the in-person preaching of the Armstrongs. A premium was also put on good food and recreation.

Gerry received permission to use college facilities to produce his paper from a minister/faculty member named Robinson, and apparently everything was okay. With the help of myself and a few other students he solicited advertising, produced articles and photos and laid it all out. We had it printed off campus, and at the start of the Feast we deposited a supply of the *Festival Courier* at a strategic location in the Feast Administration Building, a spot that almost everyone would pass. We didn't charge for the paper but provided a box for donations.

To our amazement, another minister/faculty member, who was in charge of coordinating the Feast, confiscated the donation money and ordered us to remove the papers from the building. We attempted to take this shock in stride, setting up our stack of papers elsewhere. Did the money upset him? He wouldn't say, so we guessed, dispensing with donations. Since the paper had Robinson's blessing, we assumed it was all right to continue distribution. But almost immediately the coordinator discovered our new location, confiscated the papers themselves and had them burned! Except as an overt exercise of power for its own sake, we could see no reason for this violent reaction. We were outraged, feeling righteously provoked and eager to protest. Then the other shoe dropped. Robinson now denied giving permission. He betrayed Gerry, lying to protect his own position in face of the ire of the higher-ranking Feast-Coordinator.

Gerry appealed to the college's disciplinary committee, and when it became clear to the chairman (also a minister/faculty member) that the issue boiled down to whether Gerry was lying or Robinson—a minister—was, the meeting was promptly adjourned. Gerry was offered no apology, and, clearly, if any assumptions were going to be made about who was lying, he would bear the onus. For Gerry it was the final disillusionment with "God's college" and "God's church." In a few weeks he was gone.

I harbored a lot of respect for Gerry's knowledge and intelligence, and his departure left me with grave doubts about the teachings and policies of the WCG. If he thought it was all wrong, then maybe . . . But I was afraid. Where could I turn? If the Truth wasn't here, then where? Again, who was I to question all those ministers—grown men who had studied their Bibles for years? I worried, prayed, studied, fasted—agonizing over my doubts. Before he left, Gerry mentioned the rumors that field ministers had defected, taking portions of their congregations with them. Bits of information had filtered into AC about people leaving the WCG in large numbers over matters of doctrine and in protest of abuses of power by the church hierarchy. Members felt ripped off and misused. The figure of 1000 "dissidents" and/or "heretics" was heard and incredulously dismissed. Impossible! And yet . . .

But on January 5, 1974, I gave up. I was tired of wondering, doubting, *thinking*. It was hard, painful work. I missed the days of comfortable, uncomplicated certitude. I was nostalgic for the feeling of totally accepting and being accepted—of being loyal to and swept up by a movement and obeying without question. I wanted reassurance, that old sense of security and cosmic validation. Enough of hassle and mental gymnastics!

That was the day Deputy Chancellor Ron Dart returned from a ministerial conference at headquarters in Pasadena and reported to the AC congregation that all was well with the Work. Yes, there were dissident ministers and members scattered across the country (the first official confirmation we had heard), but they were simply wrong. They were apostates, "fallen away," and in the grip of misconceptions and falsehoods. Their falling away had been prophesied in the Bible, and it was merely another step in God's Plan. It was an expected development, necessary to the End Time flow of events leading to the return of Christ. It was a wonder it hadn't happened sooner, really. The defections were streamlining the organization. We were collectively "throwing up," getting rid of what was bothering us. We could now stop doubting and questioning and get on with the Work. Personally, Dart said, he was delighted and encouraged.

So was I. Dart convinced me, and I felt revived. After the sermon I told a friend that it was "the end of an era." I was through with criticism and heresy. I was determined to renew my loyalty to the organization. In retrospect I'm appalled. What happened to me? Was I really just *tired*? Is that what is meant by the "banality of evil?" Is mere fatigue and laziness enough reason to set aside doubt and honest disputations? Was I, as a more or less normal human, so constructed that mental (and physical) comfort was more important than free-

dom and inquiry? Was I re-convinced that "an open mind would be
filled by Satan" as one of the ministers had preached? Could I forget
about Chapman, Robinson, Gerry, the ashes of the *Festival Courier*,
and all my legitimate questions?

Yes. For about two weeks. That was the last hurrah of my faith
based on fear. A part of my mind launched one last, desperate attempt to be anesthetized, and then I broke loose for good.

A fellow member of the erstwhile "heretical underground"
visited one of the dissident churches, a congregation in nearby
Shreveport, Louisiana. On January 21, he gave me a three-hour re-
port, detailing the disputes over doctrine, and revealing the cover-
ups about misuse of funds and personal sins and indiscretions of the
hierarchy. He told of Dr. Martin, a respected minister and theological
researcher in Pasadena who had left the WCG and was now producing reams of Biblical material that effectively assailed nearly
every major church doctrine. As he talked—animatedly and earnestly—I experienced what I can only describe as a suspended, "wa-
tery" sensation. My mind seemed to melt, flowing away from "me" in
all directions. As my friend poured forth with revelation after revelation, undermining my recently renewed sense of utter belonging, I
was briefly cast into a vortex of terrifying confusion. On one level I
was out of control, panicky and distraught. I didn't want to hear this!
But it had the ring of truth, the undeniable clamor of suppressed
veracity. On another level, all was calm and rational. I realized a decision had to be made, an incontrovertible step must be taken. I
vacillated between these levels, as if scrambling for balance on the
edge of some black and final pit. It was, I supposed, a "moment of
truth."

And toward the end of the three hours the decision came. It
was a sudden event (though long prepared for, albeit inadvertently).
From a deep "somewhere" I sensed a focusing—a perception on the
borderline between the physical and the mental. An entire tapestry
of half-awareness resolved into sharp perspective. All the doubts,
questions, rumors, and criticisms finally surfaced together, unen-
cumbered by fear. There was a glow of understanding: *I was a free
individual before God and I had been duped.* I felt a tremendous release,
as if manacles had fallen from my wrists or a blindfold slipped from
my brow. As if a hypnotist had snapped fingers to bring me out of
a trance.

But a kernel of apprehension remained. I needed to confirm
my freedom. I needed to act, to walk as if the shackles and blinders
were gone. Five days later I traveled to Shreveport myself. In the
morning, some friends and I attended Sabbath services at the local
WCG, listening with those who were still in the fold, as a minister
dispatched from AC delivered an ultimatum to the congregation.

Apparently there were some who were still torn between staying and leaving. They were attending the WCG in the morning and then showing up at the dissidents' services in the afternoon. The minister told them they must decide—now. Those who refused to unequiv-ocally choose loyalty to the Armstrongs would be "disfellowshipped," that is excommunicated, and thus automatically sentenced to eternal death in the Lake of Fire. As to the excesses of the power-hungry hierarchy, the minister said: "I'm sorry, but I don't apologize." (And, he might have added, hate is love, war is peace, and ignorance is knowledge. George Orwell would have recognized this guy.) In closing, the man said, "It's all a matter of government, God's or Satan's." The battle lines were clearly drawn. As in all religious con-flict, you were for or against; there was no breathing space in the middle.

In *The True Believer* Eric Hoffer wrote: "All active mass move-ments strive . . . to interpose a fact-proof screen between the faithful and the realities of the world. They do this by claiming that the ulti-mate and absolute truth is embodied in their doctrine and that there is no truth nor certitude outside it."

When we strolled into the dissident services that same after-noon, the difference was immediately obvious. The WCG people had been gripped by fear. They had been hesitant to speak, with-drawn and cold. Their unsmiling eyes looked as if they were peering between bars. They were distrustful and nervous. In contrast, the afternoon people were warm, friendly, and eager to discuss the issues at hand. They were in that flush of the first love of freedom: righteous rebellion. There was a zeal for openness and fresh thoughts. They were compelled to be there, but only by a desire to explore and dis-cover. In the morning I had heard people ridicule and castigate former friends who had left the WCG and submitted to the "bonds of Satan." In the afternoon I heard people speak of tolerance, pati-ence, and the extension of good will. I was exhilarated by the courage and loving attitude dispayed by these rebels. They believed the morning folks were wrong, but there was no apparent bitterness. They spoke of them not as "lost," condemned souls, but as wayward children who were perhaps being a little silly for the moment. There would always be room for them when they came around in their own good time.

This idyllic attitude—an almost utopian state of affairs—wouldn't survive intact on an organized basis (such seems to be im-possible), but individuals had been freed and enlightened, and many would remain that way. To be temporarily in the midst of this col-lective zeal for positive change was a rare privilege. I think many of those involved in this "revival" realized something very special was going on. It's rare for numbers of people to lovingly embrace drastic change.

By the end of the day my last kernel of apprehension disappeared. I had seen the contrast between fear and love expressed by real people with my own eyes. I was *out* of the WCG. But since I was only a few months from graduation, I decided to stick it out at AC and obtain my diploma (even though it would be unaccredited).

I returned to Shreveport the following week, and a few days after that I was summoned to Kelly's office. As Dean of Students he had apparently been assigned the task of dealing with dissident students. He asked why I had gone to Shreveport, and I replied that I was trying to understand what was going on, trying to separate truth from falsehood. He said the dissident minister I had met was "a liar," though he admitted he had never spoken with the man. We discussed differences for a while, and then he said I must decide between the WCG or the dissidents—all for, or all against, and I must do so quickly. I told him that was my own business. In the face of resistance he finally conceded my right to decide for myself ("You mean like it says in the AC Bulletin?" I asked), but requested that I not spread my views and beliefs among the student body and that I not return to Shreveport. "I can't have students going to Shreveport," he said. Indeed. There was too much to be learned.

As the number of defections among church members and ministers grew (that year about 2,000 members and forty ministers would leave), and as students and even a few faculty members left AC, those who remained (the majority) became increasingly polarized. The issues were the misuse of church funds through general extravagance and gambling (by Garner Ted), the personal immorality of some church leaders, and the major differences over basic doctrine and how crudely the differing opinions had been handled. (Usually just arbitrarily condemned and/or shouted down and/or ridiculed.)

For once there really was an "heretical underground" at AC Big Sandy, and it centered around Howard Clark. The nucleus of "membership" was all those students who made the pilgrimage to Shreveport and then, contrary to Kelly's wishes, talked about what they had learned. It seemed that every few days a new face would show up at Clark's house—another student braving social and religious ostracism in an attempt to find out what was really happening. It was a place where *any* question could be freely asked and freely answered.

There was little open conflict between dissidents and true believers, but everyone had a notion of who was who. The entire WCG organization was confused and in a state of flux, and the administration seemed to have no direct and concrete policy for dealing with those they knew or suspected to be heretics. But they incessantly preached about loyalty and apostasy, and the fears of the faithful divided the campus. The true believers implicitly (and explicitly) understood they were to avoid those who were discussing "false teaching" and who were questioning the methods and character of the Armstrongs and their lieutenants.

For example, a friend of mine named Brad wished to date a certain coed. Since she happened to be a local girl, he phoned her home to make arrangements. Her father, who worked on the AC campus and therefore knew most of the students, was livid. He forbade his daughter to go out with Brad since he knew that Brad was my friend! I had been encountering this man once or twice a week, and he had never given the slightest hint that he held such strong opinions about me and my views.

As the weeks passed I heard of more accusations and condemnations made behind my back, but no one confronted me face-to-face. Once, I walked into a dormitory lounge and without a word the six students who were sitting there immediately rose and left. I sensed the attitude: "We know you're headed for the 'bonds of Satan,' but we're not going to save you. Just get out of here so you won't trouble us with questions we can't answer and issues we won't face."

When discussions did ensue, most dissidents tried to keep them on a calm, reasonable level, taking pains to back up arguments with Biblical references. Most still accepted the Bible as the revealed word of God and just wished the organization to examine the doctrinal disputes with an open mind. That this was largely a futile hope was demonstrated by a comment from a high-ranking minister/faculty member. He asked one of my friends about what I believed. (The hierarchy had grown so devious that it may not actually have occurred to him to ask *me*.) My friend told him not to worry about me because I was studying the Bible more than anyone he knew. "Yes," replied the minister, "but *what* is he studying?" Apparently even sections of Holy Writ were now suspect. The policies of the organization had superceded even their supposed source.

On February 25 was the "Monday Massacre." Garner Ted Armstrong had flown in from headquarters in Pasadena to end confusion and marshall the forces of righteousness. On the twenty-third he had delivered a blistering sermon at Sabbath services, inflaming the faithful with fresh distrust and, in some cases, hatred for the dissidents. It was an inspired performance by a talented orator. At the end, several hundred people spontaneously leaped to their feet, cheering and waving. I had a vision of Nuremberg, 1935, and was actually frightened. I counted six of us who didn't cheer.

On the twenty-fifth, Garner Ted convened a minister's conference at AC, and, after a forty-minute opening prayer, which saw him break into sobs, he harangued and intimidated the forty or so assembled church leaders for seven hours. Several had entered the meeting with misgivings about the organization, but by the time it was over, only four still stood their ground, resisting the demand for total loyalty. They were fired from the ministry and disfellowshipped from the church.

The next day it was the student body's turn to be purified. Kelly and an associate delivered wild-eyed diatribes calling on us to "purge out those who are not willing to change!" (Everyone knew who he meant; but of course it was the dissidents who had already changed.) We were told there was a "morass of rebellion" and that the situation was "insane." The Devil was attempting to divide and conquer God's Church, and the rebels were on his side, partaking of evil. To cap it off, we were reminded that "there are things we shouldn't even think, let alone say." That was the official "amen," the end of all discussion. It was, as one of my companions whispered, "total war." He and two other dissidents quit AC immediately after the sermons. I was tempted as well—to indignantly storm out. But it was only two more months to graduation, and I decided to endure.

Shortly after, eight students visited with one of the ministers who had been canned in the "Monday Massacre." He briefed us on the power struggles within the hierarchy, the wasting of church funds, the deep divisions over what many considered to be corrupt doctrines. (Herbert Armstrong's support of "British-Israelism" was one. We had been taught that the "Lost Ten Tribes of Israel" were the modern British and Americans, the "true" Israelites.)

Next day the student body was assembled, and Kelly announced that twenty students had been fired from their campus jobs because they had contact with disfellowshipped persons. The kicker was that he wouldn't release the names of those who were "terminated." You had to guess if you were among the casualties, and, therefore, further incriminate yourself by asking for official confirmation. (As it turned out, all eight of us who had been at the former minister's house the day before were on Kelly's list, and we had reason to believe one of the eight was an informer.)

That evening I phoned Kelly to discuss my termination. He said that if I would "repent" my differences with WCG, it would save my job. I refused, and we both knew it was a de facto way of getting rid of me altogether. Without a job I couldn't afford to stay in school. I had enough credit hours to receive my degree, and all I needed was to fulfill the requirement of one class—a class taught by Kelly himself. If I agreed to leave AC then and there, would he waive that requirement and give me my degree? He refused.

The next day Kelly kicked my friend Pam out of AC. She had been on the termination list and had gone to Kelly's office to discuss her firing. She wondered why her job had been affected by a visit to a former member. Kelly replied that the salaries were paid via the donations of church members, so it was a betrayal of the brethren to use their money to pay dissidents. It would have been an appropriate moment to mention how the brethren's money had been used to buy planes, limos, jewelry, and other extravagances for the WCG hierarchy, but Pam merely said, "I don't think going to see a former minister should have anything to do with my job."

"Your job isn't to think," Kelly replied irritably. "You aren't paid to think."

"Oh, that's right," Pam countered, "Christians aren't supposed to think."

Kelly began to shout. He yelled, "That's enough!" He didn't want to hear any more. He told Pam she was expelled from AC, and, right on the spot, he instructed his secretary to file the necessary papers. As Pam left his office, he slammed the door behind her.

Clark advised Pam to take the matter before the disciplinary committee, but, before doing that, she decided to confront Kelly face-to-face one more time. The next day she returned to his office, and Kelly apologized for his outburst, though he denied having ordered her out of school. In any case, he let her back in, though still without her job.

When she was through, I went in and offered him the same deal I had a few days before. This time, appearing a little chastened and weary, he agreed. I could submit a paper to fulfill the requirements of his course and then leave school. I would return to receive my diploma on graduation day. He urged me once again to "get my head screwed on straight," and then I left.

Pam and I had been dating for several months and on May 4, we were married by Howard Clark in a simple, informal ceremony in his farm field. Since the previous December we had been growing out of the organization together, and gradually it became apparent that we were simply a natural pair. Neither of us ever actually proposed marriage—it just happened, like one stream flowing into another to make a river.

Howard's wife, Beverly, baked a cake, and I bought two cases of beer. To this day we take satisfaction in the fact that excluding the cost of the marriage license, we spent less than fifteen dollars on our wedding. We invited five fellow students and forty showed up—both dissidents and true believers. There was an unspoken truce for the duration of the event, and I warmly shook hands with or hugged several people I would never talk to again. But such can be the nature of organized religion.

Clark hired me as a laborer out on his farm until the end of May, and then we returned to AC for the commencement exercises. It was a bittersweet moment.

The "heretical underground" had grown cynical as the conflict in the WCG unfolded, and we howled in mischievous delight when we discovered that Kelly had a bidet installed in the bathroom of his house. (For the uninitiated, a bidet is a toilet-like fixture that can be used to wash your buttocks after a bowel movement.) Some began to refer to him as "Clean Ass Kelly," and mused that since so many true believers were "brown-nosers," Kelly's posterior must be scrupulously maintained in a pristine condition. We further mused about how appropriate it would be if, at the graduation ceremony, all the students bound for the field ministry would accept their diplomas and then face Kelly's back. With a practical flourish he would then drop his expensive, tailored slacks, and one by one, for the last time, they could all bend and kiss his ass.

But the real graduation ceremony was staid and anticlimactic. The only highlight was Garner Ted. As Kelly called us forth—the officer candidates of God (and their future wives)—Garner Ted Armstrong handed out the diplomas and shook our hands. He grasped my hand firmly and beamed. He didn't know me from Adam, but I *looked* like a clean-cut, properly educated product of God's college. As he said "Congratulations," his voice reminded me of his fateful radio broadcasts from years before. I beamed back. One way or another, this man and his organization had taught me a lot. I wouldn't be fooled again.

But that is not to say I wouldn't be tried.

"Life is real! Life is earnest!

Longfellow

Patrick Dwyer

Cannon Fodder

In the summer of 1974, Pam and I lived in her native Louisiana, and I took a job at a chemical plant in Baton Rouge. There was a billboard prominently displayed at the gate of the plant that read: "1,342 Days without an Injury—Think Safety!" During my first week of employment I watched it climb to 1,347. It was comforting because even a rookie like me could see this chemical plant was a gamble.

The boiled frogs tipped me off. I was sent behind a warehouse to take up miscellaneous debris and found myself on the bank of a narrow ditch filled with a brownish, viscous liquid that was crawling sluggishly toward the Mississippi, less than a mile away. The foul creek was steaming and bubbling, and as I cautiously approached I could feel it radiating heat, like some hellish tributary of the River Styx. An inveterate experimenter, I was about to dip my rake into the stream to see if it would dissolve when I saw the cooked bullfrog. It was a huge specimen, perhaps fifteen inches stretched out, and it was floating belly-up in the ditch, apparently boiled alive. Further upstream I could see another carcass flowing down from somewhere at the back of the plant. Obviously amphibians weren't included in the tally at the front gate; I had never seen anything so *injured*. Little did I imagine that I was next.

I was a member of a non-elite unit known as Temp-Timers. We were hired out to the chemical plant (and other odious locales) as temporary labor, dispatched on missions unfit or unprofitable for valuable, full-time employees. A private agency served as a clearing house and reaped a percentage of the hourly wage we earned on any given job. But I soon learned that if I desired to be "temporary" labor at the chemical plant for the rest of my useful working life—at minimum wage—I would be welcome to do so. I was twenty-three years old, and I had to wonder—did life really have the potential to become that desperate? I decided I must have inadvertently enrolled in a branch of that infamous institution, the Real World.

The entry-level course was basic: lift and carry, hustle and sweat. My instructor was a hard-bitten little foreman with a tough-sounding Scottish name I no longer recall—something starting with "Mc." But I do remember that he was a man of few words. He had a perpetual chaw of tobacco soaking in his mouth, his left cheek bulging out as if he were sucking on a baseball. If he wanted you to move a certain carton or barrel, he just spit on it, then pointed. He had an effective range of about twenty feet and was unpopular at lunchtime.

Being of average intelligence, I soon graduated from miscellaneous menial tasks to the drum-filling detail. I then stood in front of a large spigot and controlled the flow of malodorous, 400-degree (Fahrenheit) resin into fifty-gallon drums. When full, they weighed several hundred pounds and were too hot to touch with bare hands, but I had to wrestle each one out from under the spigot and move it about ten feet. I believe Dante wrote about this.

I was just growing accustomed to several minor burns per shift when I was summoned to the most exalted position of all: drum-maker. As the foreman spit all over the drum-making machine, demonstrating the fine points of operation and maintenance, I was visited by the shade of Tennyson: "Half a brain, / half a brain / Half a brain onward / All in the valley of Death / Rode the six hundred."

Whoever had fabricated this mad device was a sadist. Clumsy as I was, I knew I was doomed.

The disassembled resin drums arrived at the plant in three pieces: a top, a bottom, and a cylindrical body, all with their rims pre-bent in an esoteric sheet metal fold. I had to take a top and a bottom and stick them each on a wheel. These wheels faced each other, perfectly aligned (theoretically), about three-and-a-half feet apart. I switched on the machine, and the wheels began to spin at 300 revolutions per minute. I took a cylinder and gingerly slipped it between the whirling top and bottom. There was only a couple of inches clearance, and it was a nerve-racking process. A careless move could send the pieces flying into your face. When the cylinder was positioned just so, I held it steady with my left hand and pulled a lever with my right that eased the spinning wheels into contact with the stationary cylinder. If done properly, the folds meshed at high speed and were automatically crimped, producing a sealed drum. I then pushed the lever up at the critical moment and kicked the tumbling drum off the machine with my left foot. If done improperly, that is if the cylinder was not *precisely* aligned, the drum would crumple in on itself with a horrible, tortured screech and leave the vicinity at high velocity. You had to hope you weren't in the way when it departed. *Most* of the time it would go the other way.

It was fear of this deadly contraption that led to the accident. On my second day as a drum-maker, one of the cylinders began to crumple, threatening to wing off like an artillery projectile. I jumped to the right, out of the line of fire, and my unattended right hand flopped onto the machine. It was immediately snapped up by two steel rollers that were part of the crimping system. My leather glove was ripped apart, and all four of my fingers started to disappear into the mechanism. The pain was shocking. The monster's switch was on the wall, just above my right shoulder, and I clawed at it with my left hand. But stretching across my chest from the left, I couldn't reach it—I was about two inches short—and no amount of frenzied straining could close the gap. I could feel the wetness of blood on my fingers.

I was yelling, bellowing out in pain, terror, and frustrated rage. One of my fellow grunts rushed in from the next room, hit the switch, then instantly yanked my hand out of the rollers. My middle finger was shredded.

At the hospital they found the bones were okay, so they stitched the mess together, and a week later I returned to the plant. In spite of the momentary anguish, I was embarrassed by my mishap, upset that I had ruined the 1,300+ days of injury-free operation. But on the way in I noticed that the total at the front gate was now up to 1,355. I had expected to see a single digit. Well, maybe they had just forgotten to change the numbers. But then I also noticed one of the other Temp-Timers was sporting a bandaged finger. I was suspicious, but I approached the foreman anyway, saying how sorry I was to have spoiled that exemplary string of safe days.

He stared at me quizzically. I guess he was trying to determine if I was joking. When he saw I was sincere, he spit and burst into laughter.

"That safety record," he chortled, "is for the regular employees. *You* guys are dropping like flies!"

The next day the tally was up to 1,356. End of Lesson One.

"There is no ancient gentleman but gardeners, ditchers, and grave makers; they hold up Adam's profession."

Shakespeare

Mark Coyle

Sons of Ditches

For the next few years I pursued various blue-collar jobs, relishing the notion of being a member of Labor, a hard-working grunt
helping to construct and maintain the infrastructure of the community. I enjoyed the role of "noble ditchdigger," an attitude fostered by some of my experiences at Ambassador College. I proudly
recall the day when I turned down an honor.

I was sitting in the office of the Assistant Director of Data Processing, and he was offering me a position. Data Processing (D.P.)
was a prestige outfit on campus. Since every student worked for the
college, there was a wide range of possible assignments. You could
end up scrubbing toilet bowls, mopping floors, policing rain gutters,
washing dishes, or, as I was doing, digging ditches. However, if certain authorities smiled upon your efforts (or looks, or connections), you could be transferred to something more dignified, like
the exalted sanctum of D.P.

"How would you like to be a computer operator?" the Assistant
Director asked me. He grinned like an obsequious old uncle whose
pockets are stuffed with candy. He caught me off guard. When I
had received the summons to his office I had assumed we were going

to discuss my performance in his programming class. I was producing something considerably less than virtuoso work, and I expected an inquiry into my lack of enthusiasm for, and expertise in, RPG II. Instead he offered to hire me. I don't know, maybe he saw potential. In any case, I knew that from the operator's job I could move up to programmer, from there into systems analysis, and perhaps into management. It was an excellent opportunity. It was the kind of situation that could channel me into a promising, lucrative white-collar career. It was essentially a paid education in data processing, the wave of the future. And I would automatically gain the admiration and respect of my peers.

I smiled at the Assistant Director and said, "No thank you, sir."

He stared at me. "What?" He was genuinely taken aback. "Where do you work now?"

"On the Line Crew."

"What do you do?"

"I dig ditches." His nose wrinkled and his eyes seemed to draw back in his head. "Look," I went on, "I appreciate your offer, but I'd rather stay on the Line Crew."

The man was offended. As far as he was concerned I had ceased to be (or never was) a normally functioning human. He looked through me to the door beyond, as if I were some sort of incorporeal, fetid miasma—something awful that the janitor had overlooked. I was curtly dismissed—physically and mentally (I later got a "C" in his class)—and as I stepped out of his office I heaved a great sigh of relief. Whew! That was a close one. I had almost been promoted out of one of the best jobs on campus.

To outsiders the Line Crew didn't appear a plum assignment. Our mission was to install and maintain underground pipes—water lines, sewers, storm drains. We spent a lot of hours in wet ditches, wielding picks and No.2 shovels. We were the civil engineers' infantry—sappers and grunts. We faced danger. My first day on the crew, the foreman popped the cover on a fifteen-foot manhole and told me to descend and inspect it for damage. I was two or three feet down when he said, "Oh, by the way, you'll need this." He handed me a ball-peen hammer. "What's this for?" I asked. He grinned and replied, "That's to kill the black widows." I took a closer look and sure enough, the hole was lively with venomous spiders. It was an informal initiation rite.

Upon my admission to Ambassador College the personnel department had asked me what kind of campus job I would prefer. They were merely being polite; people were assigned where they were needed. After all, no one actually aspired to the urinal detail. But I requested "hard outdoor work," and that's precisely what I got. (My theory was that rigorous manual labor would provide a refreshing counterpart to academic pursuits. It did.)

On the Line Crew I found a niche. Amidst the sweat and dirt (and black widows), I discovered a new world—a subterranean network of pipe, cable, conduit, and wire. I was introduced to the basics of modern life, the essential circulatory system of society that's been taken for granted by three or four generations of Americans. Even on a small college campus that supported about five hundred people, the buried grid of services was omnipresent. Part of its fascination was that the uninitiated, that is, nearly everybody, had little concept of its scope, or even its existence. Unbeknownst to them, citizens were constantly walking or driving over man-made underground streams—smooth little tunnels flowing full with water, sewage, or natural gas. The electromotive force that powered their world was channeled lightning beneath their feet, shooting through insulated cable. The inocuous dirt was interlaced with a web of information as the electrical impulses of telephone transmissions coursed along wires under the sod. Civilized, settled ground is alive with the ebb and flow, pressure and force, vibrations and frequencies of human effort and design. Like sprawling forests, modern cities are supported by an expansive and intricate system of roots.

It was the sheer necessity of these roots that bolstered Line Crew morale. What was more important than the water system? More critical than the sewage system? If a life-sustaining water main ruptured, we were there to repair it, no matter the hour or the weather. When a new building needed a sewer line, we were there to construct it. (And like doctors, we "buried all our mistakes.") As student workers we logged twenty hours per week, and by the end of the first semester I had learned more on the Line Crew than I had in class. I knew how to: hold the grade for a sewer line, install a fire hydrant according to code, repair a split in a PVC water line, place valves and decide how many to use, appropriately block elbows and tees, read an engineer's schematic, and, not the least, how to properly handle a shovel. Years later, and a half a continent away, the foreman on another job saw me working in a ditch and asked "Where'd you learn how to use a shovel?" I told him. "Well," he said, "a lot of folks don't know." Of course a lot of folks don't need or even want to know and may safely journey from cradle to grave without ever touching the venerable No. 2. But a shovel to a line crewman was like a rifle to a soldier or a scalpel to a surgeon—it was the symbol of our trade, our primary hand tool. It kept us close to the earth. (And out of D.P.)

We felt effective. What greater satisfaction than to assiduously lay 2,000 feet of pipe and then turn on the water for the first time, extending the reach of the essence of life—with no leaks. Our dedication and sense of mission communicated itself to others. One day some theology student used a finger to trace a message in the dust on the door of our pickup. Instead of the tiresome "wash me," we saw simply: "II Kings 3:16." We looked up the scripture and read: "Thus saith the Lord: fill this valley with ditches." It was a decade before the Blues Brothers, but we were on a "mission from God."

And pipelines will provide some strange missions. There was one two-inch water line on campus that traversed a lake to service a campground. The plastic pipe hung suspended in the water about six feet below the surface. It was a bogus setup, defensible only because it was a "temporary" arrangement. The campground portion of the water system had been plagued with persistent leakage, and the engineers theorized there was a bad joint somewhere in the lake section of the line.

Mac, our foreman, secured a small pontoon boat, and one sunny afternoon we cast off for subaqueous adventure. We found the line, and my fellow crewman, Mike, and I stripped to our underwear and jumped in. Since the line was pressurized at sixty pounds per square inch, our plan was to take turns diving down to the pipe, swimming along it and feeling for the leak. It was most likely to be at a joint, and the outrushing of water would be obvious.

Fortunately the line was laid across a narrow portion of the lake, and it required only about thirty joints of pipe to span it. Still, by the time we had struggled down to each one, and checked the rest of the line as well, we were exhausted. And we found no leaks. We flopped back onto the deck of the boat like a couple of spent bass, and Mac revved up the twenty-five-horse outboard and headed for the dock. But Mike and I were too close to the bow, and, when we hit a choppy area, the pontoons dipped below the surface, submarining. A wave washed over the deck, and for one startling moment we were diving for the bottom. Mike and I jumped back, and the pontoons immediately broke the surface and returned to an even keel. But Mike's pants, complete with wallet, had been swept overboard, and without thinking he vaulted the rail to retrieve them.

As soon as the deck was inundated, Mac had cut the engine. He was a native of Kansas, a son of the prairie, who in all his forty plus years had never learned to swim. He had been jittery all day—afraid of the lake, afraid of the boat, and especially afraid of that raucous, churning outboard motor. These were all alien to this Kansas farmboy—unnatural, unsettling. If God had intended for people to be messing around in the water, He would have given them fins, gills, and watertight nostrils—or like Jesus, we would all be able to walk on top. A stock tank was the biggest body of water with which Mac was comfortable.

So when the pontoons tried to dive for periscope depth, Mac was terrified. His worst fears were confirmed. The boat would sink and he would drown; and it would serve him right for ever leaving

Kansas. But he probably would have calmed himself if Mike hadn't started thrashing about. He reached his pants, grabbed them and then began to flail at the waves. He said later he was only trying to tread water while he made sure his wallet was still in the pants pocket, but to Mac the situation was obvious: Mike was drowning. I admit that for a moment he did look as if he was having difficulty. I prepared to dive in after him, but Mac said no, he'd run the boat over. That was sensible, so I just crouched on the deck and waited to offer Mike a hand when we drew alongside.

But Mac was agitated, flustered beyond the capacity of his motor skills. At first he couldn't start the engine, and that wired him up even more. I was just about to swim after Mike anyway when the outboard roared to life—at full throttle. We were only about twenty yards from Mike and aimed right at him. The boat lurched off at high speed and jolted Mac to yet another level of anxiety. For a moment he lost control of the boat. I watched in helpless horror as we bore down on Mike like a brace of torpedoes. In three seconds we were on him, and I'll never forget his shocked, unbelieving expression as we ran him down.

He flashed under the deck, bracketed by the pontoons and heading for the bloodthirsty prop at the rear. But he had the presence of mind to reach up with one hand and grab the lip of the deck as it shot over his head. (His other hand still grasped his pants.) All I could see was his four white fingers, like some terrible claw, clutching the deck. I was just lunging to grab his arm when Mac managed to cut the engine. We yanked Mike aboard, unhurt, but at least ten years older. We sat on the deck and shuddered—aghast at what might have been. Mac was so shaken that it was impossible to be angry with him. It was the Line Crew's first and last amphibious operation. If the engineers needed frogmen, let them call Lloyd Bridges.

As tradesmen and laborers, we always had a love/hate relationship with engineers. A good engineer is priceless. He or she can save you work, teach you tricks and provide hands-on assistance when disaster strikes. Whether designing a sewer line or a bridge, a good engineer will strive for the *elegant* solution to a problem. An engineer's calculator and drawing board are practical tools, to be used in a sparing, efficient manner. They don't function as arcane instruments to aid in the generation of superfluous complexity, to show off everything an engineer almost learned at good old Tech.

But industry is cursed with an abundant supply of bad engineers—engineers as lords and wizards. Their calculators are magic wands. Poof!: obscurity. And if the system breaks down, call in the grunts to fix it and take the rap. And never, ever ask a non-engineer for advice. Just because a guy has been installing and repairing pipelines for thirty years doesn't mean he knows anything about pipe. He probably wouldn't know a trigonometric function if it crawled into his shorts.

That's the attitude that inspires tradesmen to daydreams of homocide. A bad engineer is a barnacle on the butt of progress, a loose bolt on the tail section of civilization—in effect, a saboteur. Bad engineers are produced by two factors: ignorance and swagger. It's not ignorance of engineering (though some have certainly been mutilated by trigonometry) but rather ignorance of some everyday physics: how a shovel works, how fast a backhoe digs, the limitations of the human back, why machines break down and how they're repaired, or the proper wrench for a given bolt. Each may be a trivial variable in itself, but the accumulated weight of an engineer's practical oversights can turn a project into slapstick theater.

I once worked as a water treatment plant operator (a natural outgrowth of the Line Crew experience), and there encountered a classic engineer's foible. One plant procedure required the operator to open and close a sixteen-inch valve. That's a big unit, though if properly designed it can be easily manipulated by hand. But no, some engineer decided to multiply the installation and maintenance costs by a factor of at least ten and design an air-operated valve control system. Instead of an operator spinning a wheel or working a simple lever—a foolproof system that would require a minute or two and not enough calories to power a chickadee—the operator merely had to push a button. Thousands of dollars and man-hours were added to the cost of the project to save two minutes of an operator's time and deny him a little beneficial exercise. It was beautiful (read: complex and costly) and it worked fine for almost a whole year. But the designer had forgotten (or never known) that although his drawing board was impeccable, the real world is full of dust, rust, grime, and inevitable malfunctions.

The control system was powered by an air compressor that was not only expensive to run but, due to the heavy work load, was also prone to breakdowns. As a result of one disjunctive episode, the compressor blew lubricating oil into all the plant's air lines. The delicate control system seized up. It was like dumping sand into a carburetor. The system was painstakingly repaired (by the grunts), but traces of oil would remain in perpetuity. This oil attracted dust and dirt like flies to dung, and the sensitive air-driven mechanisms would continually bind up.

So there I would be, poised in front of a polished, high-tech console—like something off the bridge of the Starship *Enterprise*. Before me were an impressive array of dials, lights, buttons, and gauges. When it was time to activate, that is open, a valve, I would push a button—the very symbol of the labor-saving twentieth century—and then run like hell. I had to dash down a long corridor, scoot down two flights of stairs, whip through two doors, hang a sharp right down another long hallway and then leap onto a twelve-foot stepladder (pre-positioned). At the top I would pull the cover off the valve control mechanism and feel inside for a little threaded wheel. Using two fingers, I'd spin it rapidly to the right. A loud hiss of "manual" air power indicated the valve was opening. I'd hustle back upstairs to watch the gauges. And notice: it was I who looked like an idiot, not the bastard who bequeathed me the system.

The basic philosophy of ignorant engineering is that if something *can* be done, then it *should* be done. It's the attitude that produces not only unnecessary air-controlled valves, but also three-billion-dollar nuclear power plants that no one can afford to finish building, much less operate. ("Power too cheap to meter," they said.) Before being admitted to good old Tech, a would-be engineer should be required to provide evidence of prolonged contact with the real world. For example, take a farm boy who's used baling wire and chewing gum to keep a 1946 John Deere running for a decade, and then teach him to be elegant. You'll have a top-shelf engineer.

Ignorance is curable (or avoidable), but swagger is often terminal. Even a competent engineer is a curse if he's also a power-hungry martinet. Usually the demands of politics and self-aggrandizement negate technical skill. And many good engineers have been ruined by being charged with purely administrative duties. Exalted beyond the field and the drawing board, their structural aptitudes coalesce into a kind of rigid mathematical authority, and they begin plugging people into equations. Worse is the calculating menace who went into engineering solely to achieve a management position. From square one he aimed not for superior design and technical implementation, but rather for control, power, and prestige. These schemers regard tradesmen and laborers as inferior beings and treat them as such. They do the most damage when they're still rising through the lower ranks. (Later, when they're at the pinnacle of power, ensconced in some plush office, their command decisions can often be ignored or circumvented by those out in the trenches.) In the field they practice abusing what authority they have in order to prepare for even greater authority. It's best to avoid them, or failing that, bludgeon them with a theodolite.

On the Line Crew, most of our contact with engineers was through their drawings. Every pipeline and all its fittings were carefully mapped for future reference, and before digging we always studied the schematics. It was embarrassing to be looking for a water main and cut a telephone line in the process; Ma Bell was always testy when it came to interrupted phone service. The drawings were usually accurate, but sometimes you could lose half a day searching for a line that the engineer said was so many feet from thus and such, when in reality it was at least ten feet further south, north, or whatever. Ten feet is a long way when you're digging by hand. (In Texas the pipes were shallow, and we did a lot of handwork.)

So when plagued by a "missing" pipe or valve, we employed our secret tool: "witching" rods. They scared Mac to death—he figured it was demons at work—and he forbade us to use them. But our colleague Bill always kept a pair hidden in the truck, and, when we couldn't find a line, we would slip them out when Mac wasn't around. Our divining tools were L-shaped lengths of brass brazing rod, twenty-five inches long, with five inches bent over to form a handle. You'd hold a rod in each hand, gently pinched between thumb and forefinger, the rods level, parallel and about a foot apart. You'd walk slowly around the area in question until the rods came together and crossed. When they started to move you could hold them back only with deliberate, concentrated effort—they swung together by themselves. I was astonished the first time I tried it, and it worked more often than not. When the rods crossed, you stopped and sighted down between them, and there was an excellent chance that the missing pipe was right there. I've seen it theorized that witching has something to do with electromagnetic attraction, but it's definitely a fringe area, and most scientific authorities consider it to be, ahem, highly suspect. Whatever. I've seen it work too many times to be mere chance, but even so, when we used the rods we made sure there were no witnesses. (Years later, at another job, the crew I was on used a patented magnetic device for locating valves and lines, but it didn't work as well as the rods and, unlike them, couldn't detect plastic or cement pipes. When all else failed, we would look both ways then pull out my rods.)

I finished college with a BA in theology and a lot of experience with pipelines. I've never spent time in a pulpit, but I've seen the bottom of a lot of ditches. Back in Northern Minnesota I hired on with a city water department and took up graduate field work. I realized the sandy, shallow ditches of East Texas were a luxury compared to the toilsome excavations of the Frost Belt. Northern water lines had to be buried a minimum of seven feet to prevent freezing, and the "soil" consisted of either solid rock or tight clay. The occasional ditch in sand was a real treat, a gift from below.

Because of the ledge rock, we had to do a lot of blasting, and, because of the blasting, we had to do a lot of jackhammering—drilling holes for dynamite. I always liked running a jackhammer; it was romantic. Whenever you see a TV commercial that wishes to portray a macho, blue-collar dude who *earns* his money (or beer or deodorant or pain-killer) you see some brawny hulk wrestling with a jackhammer. There's a genuine sensation of power when one presses the air lever on a big hammer and it starts to buck and roar. Spending a few hours boring through rock or chipping pavement gives one an intimate grasp of the terms "hard" and "work." It's easy for me to become lost in the relentless, incorrigible pounding—to start believing that passers-by are casting admiring, respectful glances in my direction. Not everyone gets to run a jackhammer in this life. And when one begins to feel blessed, it's been running too long.

But even more glamorous was the blasting. It's both sobering and exhilarating to be cruising around in a pickup with twenty sticks of dynamite on the front seat. Handling powder can make one religious—not as a fearful supplicant, but as a high priest—a powerful and privileged mediator between men and Almighty Explosives. Our sense of responsibility was magnified by the fact that we detonated our charges within city limits. It was delicate business, but our blaster was an artist. Once we had uncovered the rock, Lenny would climb down into the ditch and conduct a close survey. He would scan the rock like a prospecting geologist, sometimes calling for more dirt to be excavated here and there so he could get a better look. He had learned his trade in the iron mines and knew how to read bedrock. Searching for likely cleavage areas and studying the general lie of the formation, he would carefully mark the drill holes and tell us precisely how deep to go. Then he had to decide how strong a charge at a given point would shatter the maximum amount of rock with a minimum risk to the neighborhood. When the holes were ready, he would use his pocket knife to cut a stick of dynamite into the appropriate portion—eyeballing the length. With deft, steady hands he would gently insert the blasting caps into the powder and neatly splice the leads to our blasting wire. He would ease the charges into their holes, then slowly fill them with dirt and tamp them with a wooden baton. We would drag some thick rubber mats (old conveyor belting scrounged from the mines) over the holes and then string the wire back to our pickup. We didn't have a fancy plunger-style detonator—like the one Alec Guiness fell on in the last scene of *The Bridge on the River Kwai*. Instead, Lenny liked to touch the leads to the posts of our truck's battery. When everything was ready to go, we would pile dirt on top of the rubber mats. This was our defense against shrapnel, and, therefore, the volume was critical. We wanted enough overburden to keep the blast safe, but it was senseless to dump too much since it all had to be removed later. It was a subjective judgement that Lenny had learned to make via years of experience.

One day we were blasting rock for a water main extension, and our charges were set less than a hundred feet from two residences. Lenny directed a loader operator to put three buckets of fill on top of the mats. The man dumped two and said it was enough. "No it's not," replied Lenny, "we need three." The operator was obstinate; he insisted that two buckets were sufficient. Lenny's face grew dark, but he wasn't going to argue with stubborn ignorance. He strode to the truck and pressed the wire leads against the battery terminals.

The explosion lifted the two loads of dirt about five feet straight up, and we saw one of the mats rise and flop over to one side. Small splinters of bedrock rained down, but we all watched, transfixed, as a jagged chunk of stone about the size of a grapefruit flew high out of the ditch in a long, lazy arc and crashed through the roof of a nearby garage. Lenny fired a sharp glance at the loader operator, then walked over to the residence to reassure the owner about the city's liability coverage. The next time Lenny asked for three buckets he got them.

Lenny was also a thawing expert. Before joining the department I would never have guessed how to thaw a frozen underground water line. If told, "You use a welder," I would've entertained an incoherent image of shooting sparks and melting copper. In reality, we employed a large, 400-amp welding machine to charge the frozen piping with an electric current, juicing it up like the coils in an electric heater. At that amperage, we needed only a half-hour to render a couple hundred feet of three-quarter-inch copper pipe too hot to touch.

It was simply done. We'd take the ground clamp of the welder and snap it onto the nearest fire hydrant. The "stinger"—the business end of the welder—was stuck at the terminus of a frozen stretch of line, usually where the pipe entered a house through the basement floor. That would complete the circuit, and we would switch on the welder and let it cook. There would be water running in twenty minutes or less.

One cold afternoon, Lenny and I—knights in dirty coveralls—were dispatched to a house with a frozen water line. It was routine. I dragged the ground clamp down to the fire hydrant on the corner while Lenny pulled the stinger into the basement. It was near quitting time and we were anxious to get it done and head back to the shop.

But Lenny beckoned me inside; we had a problem.

Our normal procedure was to decouple the water meter from the rest of the plumbing and disconnect the breaker box ground wire that was usually clamped to the piping near the meter. This created a clean break in the system and prevented current from our welder running all through the house. But some people don't like the looks of pipes, wires, and meters, so they improve their basements and hide it all behind partitions and paneling. We hated that. It meant we often had to mount a time-consuming meter hunt. (Many homeowners can't tell you where it is, and only their meter-reader knows for sure.) That was the situation in this house.

Lenny and I found some piping between the joists that was still exposed and traced it back to the meter. The unit was tucked into a dark, cramped corner, hidden by paneling. A small trap door in the wall provided just enough access for a hand and a flashlight. As a bonus we had to lean over and bend around a large, brand-new color television that was sitting in front of the trap door.

Lenny, an eighteen-year veteran of such obstacle courses, had developed a set of rules. Near the top of the list was: *never* unilaterally move furniture or appliances to get at a meter. He believed it would be presumptuous and intrusive for a government employee to be rearranging private possessions. In a case like this, he would outline the problem to the owner and then either have them move the stuff or get permission for us to do it. In this particular situation that was impossible. When we arrived, the woman who owned the place was on her way out the door, and we had no idea when she would be back.

There was no way we could decouple the meter without moving the TV and possibly enlarging the trap door, so Lenny's first impulse was to leave the line frozen until the next day. That was the correct strategy; deep down we both knew it.

But: 1) Having traveled there and deployed our welder, we wanted to complete the job and round out our shift. "Finish what you start" is one of those puritanical American proverbs pounded into our heads from the beginning. The emphasis is always on production, spawning the attitude of public servants turned cynical by trying to please the fickle public: "Do *something*, even if it's wrong." 2) We didn't want to face a thawing job first thing in the morning when the day is at its coldest. 3) If the woman returned home and found her water still frozen, she would phone city hall to raise hell. Then we would not only have to explain the situation to her, but to the bureaucracy as well. Despite logic and good sense being on our side, there was no way we would look good. We were working against the common assumption that all city employees are stupid and lazy, and no one would believe that we had left the line frozen out of respect for the woman's TV, her paneling, her privacy, and our good manners. 4) Like most humans, we didn't believe that anything real bad could happen to us.

So, we did something stupid. Lenny told me to reach in and hook the stinger onto the meter coupling. "We'll just give it a quick shot of juice," he said. "I don't think it's froze too hard." We tramped back outside and switched on the machine.

There was a guage on the welder that should've read 400 amps. Well, it did, but only for an instant. The needle fell to 300 amps and just sat there. Our question *should* have been: "Where are those other 100 amps?" That's an awful lot of current to be missing. It was a veritable prison-break of a current drop, like several dangerous cons busting out of San Quentin.

But naturally, our first reaction was: "What's wrong with the welder?" It couldn't be anything we had done. It was like the prison guards saying, "There's something wrong with the light, we can't see the prisoners in their cells." Nothing bad can happen to us.

But after a few minutes, when it was clear there was nothing wrong with the machine, we began to get nervous. We finally asked ourselves where the 100 amps could be, and we didn't like the answer. With a sudden impulse of fear, Lenny hit the switch and killed the welder.

It was as if he had delivered a cue. The moment the welder died, a front door burst open three houses down the block. A woman charged out into the snow, screaming and crying, grasping a traumatized child in her arms. Their refrigerator was on fire. Lenny and I exchanged a horrified glance; they had found our 100 amps.

The woman didn't know that, of course; we were simply government authority figures, someone to run to. We did our best to calm her trembling, and then entered the house. A clock on the kitchen wall was smoking, and the inside of the refrigerator was pitch black. It smelled awful. I went to the utility room and found that the ground wire to the breaker box was too hot to touch. I shivered. A few more minutes of cranking with the welder and we would've burned that house down.

Lenny tried to explain to the woman what had happened, tried to make sense of it, and, of course, he couldn't. She understood perfectly. "Why did you turn on that machine," she asked, "if you knew you shouldn't?" Indeed. She was convinced we were dangerous idiots. She was wrong. We were dangerous because we were normal—trying to balance right, wrong, and expediency; trying to please everyone and ourselves too—*normal* idiots. They're everywhere.

But Lenny was usually confident and competent, and it was contagious. It buoyed the crew on those sub-zero nights when we were called out for emergency water line repairs. There are few vistas more melancholy than the view from the lip of a flooded ditch on a wicked winter night. On cold, black evenings like that I often wondered what the local programmers and systems analysts were doing. I could picture the Assistant Director of D.P. perched on the edge of the freezing, muddy trench, smirking and holding up a print-out fresh off the IBM 360/22. Some warm, dry programmer has directed the machine to print, in large block letters: DUMB SHIT. The Assistant Director waves it at me, then purposely drops it and watches gleefully as the paper wafts into the ditch and slaps the mud. Oh well, GI-GO. Given another chance, I'd probably still opt for the ditches.

Those wretched jobs had their special rewards. One night I was trying to locate a serious rupture in a six-inch water main. The ditch was eight feet deep, and a bad valve upstream was allowing so much water to seep into the hole that our pump couldn't keep up. I was bent over in two feet of icy water, feeling along the line to assess the damage. Numerous cave-ins had prolonged our digging (and re-digging) for four hours. I was plastered with cold mud and soaked to the skin from the waist down. It was five degrees below zero and windy, and my assistant and I were working by flashlight.

The hole was literally in some guy's backyard, and our work had cut off his water supply. He had been without the use of sinks and toilets for several hours with no relief in sight. His yard was a mess—like one huge bomb crater. Still, he walked over to the trench, gazed down at us for a minute and then shook his head.

"I don't know what they're paying you guys," he said, "but whatever it is, it ain't enough!"

Amen.

But that was not the pinnacle of my blue-collar career.

"Your shit is our bread and butter."

Anonymous

Fred Yiran

Rainy Night at the Sewage Plant

Historically speaking, it hasn't been terribly long since raw sewage flowed in the gutters of major cities. Only in the past century or so have humans taken the trouble to dispose of their bodily and industrial wastes in some sort of scientific, sanitary manner. As moderns, we pause little to ponder where that water swirling in our toilet bowls is headed. *Somebody* takes care of such scatological matters. Somebody like me; I used to do it. It was more than a job, it was a thick slice of life. The boss used to leave the plant at the end of the day and caustically intone, "Well, boys, it's been a real *slice.*"

A typical sewage plant is merely an artificial river, refined and concentrated to physically, biologically, and chemically purify the incoming sewage, which is better than ninety percent water. (As one of our training manuals sardonically noted, not even diamonds are that pure.) The treatment of domestic sewage is a relatively simple process of screening, floating, settling and encouraging natural processes of decay. The main idea is to provide a constant, healthy environment in which the bacteria in the sewage can get on with the job of breaking down the offensive materials. In principle it's simple—even beautiful, convivial: let the "bugs" do it.

145

In reality, of course, beauty departs when sewage arrives. Enter the sewage plant operator, the keeper of the river—the person who tends the machinery, monitors the flow, carries away debris and, in the process, develops immunities to several diseases rarely mentioned in polite company. His life at the plant is necessarily a routine, for he seeks consistent results day after day. He generally gets them, except on rainy nights. God save him from the rainy night.

Theoretically, a sewage plant should be immune to rainfall. In practice, however, hardly a plant in existence is unaffected by what is known as "infiltration." It's a sinister term, and for good reason. Infiltration is the seepage of ground water and rain water into sewer pipes, which carry waste to the sewage plant. The water may creep in through pipe joints, cracks in the pipe, or manholes—particularly those in low areas. During a hard, steady rain, such seepage can easily double or triple the normal peak flow, transforming a sedate graveyard shift into a frenzied nightmare. The rainy night is the *piece de repulsion* of the sewage game. Let me tell you about it.

I arrive at the plant at 10:45 p.m. It's been raining for more than seven hours. I am under no illusions. The operator on duty, looking haggard and spongy, briefs me on current conditions then gratefully departs for environs more conducive to mental and physical health. Just about anywhere else will do.

The flow meter tells me that our influent volume, the sewage coming in, is nearly three times the normal rate. It hasn't rained for some time, meaning that sewage lines all over town are being thoroughly scoured of accumulated debris. This is mostly sticks, sand, and miscellaneous refuse, but we've also received two-by-fours, dentures, flashlights, small toys, pouches of marijuana, and my personal favorite: a snowshovel! (I don't know either). The debris is now headed my way.

I slip into rubber boots and gloves and prepare myself to inspect the bar screen. The bar screen is a large steel grate of parallel bars about a half-inch apart set in the sewage influent line. It's our first line of defense and the essence of *raw*. It traps fecal matter, condoms, feminine hygiene products, dead goldfish, rags, dirty soap chunks, and, for some reason, a great number of pickles and carrots, in addition to several things that aren't readily identifiable. Our screen, nicknamed "the salad bar," is on a lower level; the odor hits me at the top of the stairs. It's not an overpowering stench but more of a gnawing unpleasantness that reeks of decay and putrefaction. I descend the greasy spiral stairs into a damp, low-ceilinged chamber. The roar of incoming sewage throbs beneath my feet—an intimidating sound.

The bar screen is mechanically raked by a chain-drive affair that scrapes the debris off the bars, lifts it into the room and dumps it into a shallow hopper. My function is to empty the hopper—with a shovel. These screened deposits are collectively called "rags." The pile before me, portions of it having spent several weeks in the sewer lines, is a sodden mass of gray-black horrors. We never look too closely at the rag hopper; we just grab a shovel and turn our head away. Usually there isn't much of an accumulation, and we get by nicely with five-gallon buckets, filling two or three per shift and hauling them up the stairs and out. Tonight, my predecessor has dropped down some 55-gallon drums. I jam my shovel into the hopper and quickly remove five scoops of utter and complete filth.

The odor escaping from the disturbed pile almost makes me retch. Normally the smell isn't quite that bad, but this stuff has been hunkering out in the sewer mains, going septic. Also, under usual daily conditions we're affected by a phenomenon known as "olfactory fatigue." Our noses, being constantly abused, lose all interest in the aroma of sewage; we don't notice it anymore. Except on occasions like this. I hurry back upstairs.

It's raining harder now. I dash to the control room to check the wet well level gauge, which will dictate the course of my life for the next eight hours. The wet well is a large holding tank under the bar screen. As it fills with incoming sewage, four pumps are activated in sequence to deliver the sewage to the rest of the plant. The tank acts as a regulator, evening out the fluctuating flow entering the plant. If the sewage level in the wet well gets too high, sewage overflows into a by-pass line that sends it directly to the creek. That makes a lot of people, and the Minnesota Pollution Control Agency, unhappy. If it rises even higher, as a result of a power outage for instance, I must flood the lower levels of the control building with sewage. I saw it happen once, the sewage spurting up through floor drains in macabre fountains and cascading down stairways like a waterfall. It made me very unhappy. Somewhere between those two disasters, a high wet well level can fill up a few basements in a low area of town. That makes a few people unbelieveably unhappy. So it's imperative that I control the level in the wet well. Beyond controlling the rain (a technology we still lack in the waste water field), all I can do is regulate the flow of incoming sewage, which enters the plant via a thirty-six-inch diameter line. There is a valve in the line that I can open and close by hand. For some bewildering reason, the valve is outside, in the rain.

All four pumps have been running for more than an hour, but the wet well gauge creeps steadily upward. I hurry out into the rain and close the thirty-six-inch valve (affectionately known as "The Thirty-Six") three turns, then run back inside to check the gauge. The needle has slowed but rises still. I run back out and give The

Thirty-Six two more turns. Back inside the gauge is steady. I'm good for now, but it's only 11:15.

The sewage plant consists of several buildings scattered over a couple of acres of unhallowed ground. I'm supposed to keep tabs on them all. Splashing through puddles, I head for my next stop, the grit building. "Grit" consists of sand, bits of eggshells, kernels of corn, cinders, and the like. These heavier materials pass through the bar screen, settle out in the wet well and are then pumped into a grit rake, which separates the grit from the water and pushes the grit into a chute, which in turn empties it into a drum. The odor in this room is literally overpowering; it's hard to breathe in there. The drum under the chute is nearly full. A full grit drum, weighing about eight hundred pounds, is no more difficult to move than any other eight hundred pound barrel. (We hoot derisively at our official job description, which says we are called upon to perform "light physical duty.") I hold my breath as long as possible and shovel the grit into an empty drum until the drum under the chute is half-empty. (A sewage plant operator would never say "half-full" early on a rainy night.) Then I beat a hasty retreat.

My next stop is the primary clarifiers, two large settling tanks where the heretofore unsettled solids settle, and where greasy scum floats. A rotating paddle nudges the scum along the surface of the clarifier and dumps it into a "scum box." The scum box, of course, is full. Using a scoop attached to a long pole, I look like a swimming pool attendant in Purgatory as I burrow into the box and deposit three or four loads into a pail. Clarifier scum has the odor and conformation of old guts. The pail comes with me as I leave, and I empty it into a drum outside.

Before proceeding on my rounds, I head back to the control room to check the wet well level. Rising again. I run out to crank down The Thirty-Six three more turns. Steady again, but so is the rain. Fortunately there's no lightning. If I were to lose power, I'd have no way to control the wet well level. Fun times.

The phone rings and I jump. I hate to hear the phone on night shift, especially on a rainy night. It could be some miserable citizen whose basement is filling with raw sewage. Those conversations are invariably unpleasant. Then there are the strange ones—like the night some sad-voiced guy called to tell me of the fight he had just had with his wife. It seems that in the heat of battle he had taken their wedding rings and flushed them down the toilet. Now, apparently having kissed and made up, he was wondering if I could possibly find them. Stifling cruel laughter (it's a dirty business), I told him the chances were about a billion to one that I would see them go by, but I would keep an eye out.

I pick up the jangling phone. Wrong number. Whew.

Back on my rounds, I check out the heat exchanger. Here, hot water—heated by burning methane gas derived from decaying sludge (decomposing solids) in the digester tank—is brought into contact with more sludge. The sludge needs to be heated to reach and maintain the optimal temperature for organic decay (eighty-five to ninety degrees in our process), which produces more methane, and thus keeps the process moving. It always amuses me to think that the same methane gas we derive from waste and burn in our mundane furnace is a significant constituent of the atmosphere of the planets Jupiter and Saturn. How nice. Any positive thought helps on the night shift.

The chief problem in the heat exchanger is that the piping tends to clog up with rags on a sickeningly regular basis. It turns out that the most efficient way to clean the pipes is with your bare hands— not exactly high tech. You need a deft touch to feel for the critical obstruction, especially around the convoluted impeller of the sludge pump, and rubber gloves are too cumbersome. (Perhaps we need surgeons' gloves; I should mention that to the boss.) But miraculously, all flows freely tonight.

The secondary clarifiers and the chlorination system also prove to be in good shape, so I hurry back to the control building. The wet well level is rising again, so it's out to The Thirty-Six for two more turns down. Steady. Reluctantly, I return to the bar screen chamber. The hopper has refilled with rags. I top off a 55-gallon drum, muscle it out of the way and roll in a new one. At the rate the rags are coming in, the grit must also be piling up; I run to the grit building. I find a full drum—and grit crammed halfway up the chute. After fifteen minutes of shoveling, hosing and shoving, I have an empty drum under the chute. It's 12:30 a.m.

In the control room, I see that the wet well level is rising again. I crank The Thirty-Six a few more turns, then rush to the bar screen and shovel more rags. The balance of the night is spent shuttling between the bar screen, the grit building, and The Thirty-Six. Somewhere in there, I find time to spot-check all the other units, raise the chlorine dosage to help disinfect the millions of gallons of sewage that are being by-passed to the creek and eat lunch.

In the morning, our lab technician will measure hydrogen-ion concentration, biochemical oxygen demand, total suspended solids, fecal coliforms, and other esoteric parameters, but on a rainy night our progress is measured in drums. Tonight's final tally: two-and-a-half drums of rags, three drums of grit, half a drum of scum.

By dawn, the rain has eased. I'm opening The Thirty-Six (a few turns at a time) when my relief man arrives. He flashes me a knowing grin.

"Rough night?" he asks.

"Shit," I reply.

It could be a grim place to work—a literal cesspool and chemical stew—the destination of hazardous wastes (PCBs, TCE, lead, mercury, etc.), pathogenic bacteria, toxic gases, and even radioactivity. I once developed a sore throat and shallow cough that wouldn't go away. I assumed it was just a cold at first, but after nearly two months with no relief, I went to the clinic for a check-up. They ran me through every procedure they could think of: blood tests, X-rays, urinalysis, lung capacity machine, and others. When it was all over the doctor threw up his hands and said he couldn't find anything wrong. As a last resort he said, "Do you think you might be exposed to anything at work?" I think he was offended when I burst into laughter.

"Doc," I replied, "I work at the sewage plant. I'm exposed to *everything!*"

Everything, including my own black humor and that of my compatriots—potentially the deadliest hazard of all. Sir William Gilbert, of the Gilbert and Sullivan opera team, wrote: "Humor is a drug which it's the fashion to abuse." And such drug abuse is what got us through years of swing shifts that reeked of shit. We were on a constant search through our little wasteland, seeking out reasons for laughter amid reasons to puke.

To outsiders, most of our jokes and pranks seemed gross and sick, but when you eat lunch at a sewage plant every day, it's easy for your sense of the appropriate to become skewed. While down cleaning the bar screen one day, I made a joyous find: a large dead goldfish, whole and relatively unblemished. I rushed upstairs, the bright orange corpse grasped in my slimy rubber glove. Two of the boys were in the control room eating lunch and chatting with a salesman, a visitor from the "real world." I strode into the room and triumphantly slapped the squishy fish onto the table before them. "I'm buying," I announced, aglow with generosity and satisfaction. "There *is* such a thing as a free lunch!"

My fellow laborers chuckled appreciatively, shielding their sandwiches from the spray. The salesman also laughed, but that's what salesmen are supposed to do—the customer is always funny. But his mirth didn't seem entirely genuine, and he looked at us with what appeared to be pity. Well, we were accustomed to the kill-joy reactions of such Philistines. The guy probably wouldn't have appreciated having his pickup truck filled with sewage sludge either. But our boss did.

My first job as a waste water plant rookie was to pilot the sludge truck. It was a 2,000-gallon tanker, a rolling and seething bucket of filth. I would back "The Unit" under a four-inch spout and then kick on a pump. It took about fifteen minutes for the truck to fill, so instead of just sitting out there and watching the thick, black liquid flow into the tank (though it could produce a strangely hypnotic effect), I would settle down in the control room and read a magazine. The problem, of course, was that I would get into an article and lose track of time. One morning the superintendent walked in, and in a nonchalant, oh-by-the-way manner he said, "Hey, Pete, how much sludge do you think the parking lot can hold?"

I looked at the clock. Damn! I'd been pumping for twenty-five minutes. As the super howled in delight, I rushed out the door to The Unit. The foul, malodorous sludge was cascading down the sides of the truck and forming a wide, bubbling pool beneath the tires. I had an awesome mess to clean up. From then on it was the super's standard line. He'd stroll into the room and say, "Hey, Pete, how much sludge do you think the parking lot can hold?" and I'd jump, running to the door to make sure. I figured it was okay, but of course I had to check. His question would inject just enough doubt. Had I lost track of the time again? Given the monotony of the job, it was easy to do.

But he kept at it too long. One Monday morning when I was particularly disenchanted with the sewage treatment game, he asked his needling question for the last time. When he left the control room to inspect a distant part of the plant, I hurried out to the sludge truck and backed it out of the way. Then I hopped into the boss's pickup and drove it under the spout. Aflame with malicious glee, I kicked on the sludge pump. When the black ooze was brimming to the top of the truck's box and starting to surge over the sides in smelly waves, I headed back through the plant and calmly approached him. "Say, Boss," I politely inquired, "how much sludge do you think your pickup can hold?" He slumped against a wall; he knew I wasn't kidding. He knew that just like virtually everyone else under his command, I'd been driven goofy enough to do it. I had to clean the pickup, but the look on his face was worth it, and he never asked me about sludge in the parking lot again.

Naturally, after years of sensory abuse, it became increasingly difficult to shock or impress our fellow shitmen. They had seen, smelled, touched, and sometimes inadvertently tasted, enough swill, offal, goop, and dregs to ruin a lifetime of lunches for the uninitiated. So that's where we often turned our mischievous attentions—to innocent visitors, lured into our dark, clammy domain by curiosity, sales, or the requirements of a biology class. Educational tours were one of our favorite targets, and we offered no quarter to the squeamish. The best place to pull a prank was in the bowels of the bar screen, our little stinking underworld "salad bar"—"groady to the max."

As mentioned, the place smelled and crawled. Everything was dirty, and the ceiling constantly dripped. It was only condensation, but the feeling of a splash on bare skin would make tourists shrivel and spit. There was almost always a couple of full drums, putrefying in place, their loads of excrement teeming with insects and worms. As people descended the stairway into that room, huddling together to avoid touching the walls, they would grimace and wrinkle their faces. Women would squeal, men would snort, and some folks wouldn't go down at all. By the time the super or his assistant launched into their esoteric spiel about the wonders of the bar screen, the mood of nervous revulsion was at a peak. People glanced quickly from side to side, afraid perhaps that some wet and furry creature was going to dart out of a dark corner or that something worse than worms were going to skitter out of a drum. This was the time for a sting.

One time we procured a relatively clean drum and placed it in the midst of three full ones. Tommy, one of our most dedicated pranksters, crawled inside, and we plopped a cover on top. The assistant super was conducting a tour for a college nursing class, and when he saw that his audience was thoroughly grossed out (no mean feat for nurses), he gestured toward Tommy's drum. "And this," he lectured, "is some of the other waste we get in here." Tommy then leaped up, blowing off the cover as he uncorked a loud yell. There was a general gasping shriek as a dozen students went straight up. Some of them could probably have initiated successful lawsuits, claiming anguish, mental cruelty, and permanent nerve damage. But I suppose they were leery of provoking such obvious weirdos.

We were usually on the offensive, trying to impress upon the taxpayers that we worked in a very bad place and were worth at least what they were paying us, if not more. Most civilians were duly awed by the alien nature of our work place, but occasionally a visitor would show up who could astonish even such jaded sensibilities as ours.

One evening, during the hated 3:00 to 11:00 shift, a middle-aged gentleman entered the plant to inquire about his dentures. It seems that shortly after dining at a local fast food restaurant, he rushed into a bathroom and threw up. (He didn't say whether he suspected a connection.) The violence of his reaction was such that he lost his upper plate, and it was somehow flushed down the commode. Dental prices being what they are, he hurried to the sewage plant in hopes of recovery and salvage.

It may seem ludicrous, but his hopes were not farfetched. It would've been possible for his teeth to flow down to the plant and be picked up on the bar screen. We had found dentures before.

The operator on duty told him this, informing him that if his plate had arrived that day, it would be in one of the two full drums down in the bar screen chamber. If he wished to dump the drums and pick through the turds, rubbers, tampons, and such, he was welcome, as long as he cleaned it all up afterwards. The operator guided him down to the drums, certain that after one glance the man would rush to make an appointment with his dentist and spread sewage plant horror stories among his friends and acquaintances. But amazingly, the man dug in with alacrity, happy for the opportunity to search for his teeth. He carefully explored the contents of both awful drums, and, failing to find his plate, he shoveled it all back in.

Even we shitmen were scandalized. We freely speculated upon the man's planet of origin. Even if he'd been lucky(?) enough to find the teeth (they apparently got hung up somewhere in the sewer system) how could he ever have put them in his mouth again? We agreed that for us, sterilization by any means would be irrelevant. Many of our former visitors—this bitter group would no doubt include dozens of our former helpers—would have found such uncharacteristic sensitivity to be ironic, if not exactly touching.

Every summer we would procure three or four temporary laborers to aid us in our glorious cause. They fell into three categories: high school and college students, welfare recipients, or "criminals" performing community service work as part of their sentence. But they were all the same to us—cannon fodder, expendable shock troops in our eternal war against sewage. These recruits knew they were in trouble when the boss would stroll into the office on their first nervous morning and say, "Well, lookee here: fresh meat!"

We always told them we would never have them do anything that we as regulars wouldn't do—at least once. And it was true, but most of the laborers didn't believe it. Imagine their incredulity when they were dispatched on a "special mission" into the wreched, otherworldly depths of the Powers Road Lift Station, otherwise universally known as "that scumsucking shithole."

A lift station is a point in the sewage collection system where raw sewage flowing toward the plant is lifted, pumped from one elevation to another. Rare is the system that can rely entirely upon gravity flow from all its customers. Variations in elevation usually demand that sewage be forced along here and there, pumped over hills, across streams, and other obstructions. A lift station is usually a simple, buried tank containing submersible pumps. Gravity flow enters one side of the tank and is pumped up and out the other side, where it later resumes a gravity flow. The whole setup isn't much bigger than a standard manhole. But occasionally there's one like Powers Road.

Powers Road was a mini-sewage plant, complete with its own bar screen. This grate was nearly fifty feet under ground in an ugly, corrosive environment that smelled of putrefaction. It was like entering a particularly dark and forbidding mine shaft. Two long, steep flights of bare concrete stairs, dimly lit, led down into the cold and wet. The steel railings were rusted hulks—only concrete could stand the con-

stant dripping and toxic-like humidity, and even that was beginning
to corrode. It was a haven for mold, mildew, and clouds of tiny flies
that always seemed to dive for the nose and mouth.

At the very bottom, poised at the gaping mouth of a twenty-four-
inch sewer line, was the bar screen. It had to be raked by hand. Here
was a niche for our helpers. We would issue them coveralls, rubber
boots, rubber gloves, and garden rakes. This last item always startled
them. Wasn't this the twentieth century—the high-tech 1980s? Yes,
but when you entered the Powers Road Lift Station you were on a
journey back through time—when men were men and barbarians
ruled. Think of the rake as Excalibur, the coveralls as chain mail;
the sewage is a dragon, come to devour the kingdom; the Holy Grail
is found in an envelope every other Friday. Have fun, we'll see you
in an hour.

Then they would rake the usual disgusting screenings into five-
gallon pails, spilling stuff onto their feet. The full pails had to be
carried back up the slippery stairs and dumped into a drum outside.
But the worst part was the furious hand-to-hand combat with soap
chunks. Soap residue built up in front of the screen, accreting and
congealing into massive gray globs peppered with black grit. Many
were twice the size of basketballs; dense, heavy, greasy, and as slick
as slime. They had to be impaled on the tines of the rakes, and awkwardly dragged out of the flow like dead pigs. Then they had to be
grasped against the body and hauled one-by-one up to the surface,
or, if one preferred, chopped into revolting pieces and shoved into
the five-gallon pails. There might be a hundred pounds worth,
bobbing grotesquely in the raw sewage, barely visible in the damp,
stinking dimness.

It was the perfect initiation rite for our summer grunts—a short,
intense boot camp to put them in the appropriate frame of mind.
Nevertheless, our attrition rate was surprisingly low. (Though a
few took one good look and never returned after lunch.) I suppose
if most of them had had a viable alternative they wouldn't have been
with us at all. By the end of the first week the average recruit was well
on his way to usefulness, developing a fearless, angry contempt for
sewage and all its subsidiary manifestations—enduring and returning
the good-natured ridicule of the regulars. We were usually a fairly
happy family. After a dirty assignment we would build morale by
showing off some of our favorite sewage plant sights—like the aerated
condoms.

The aeration tank was a large, deep pool fed by several high-
pressure air nozzles. Raw sewage was "introduced" into the tank and
thoroughly aerated, charged with billions of frothing air bubbles—
oxygen to accelerate the natural processes of bacterial action and to
break down the organic material in the waste water. But along the
way a number of prophylactics, swirling around the tank, would be

inflated by the air and float to the surface. There they would dance on the waves, filled to bursting. At any given moment there might be dozens of these inadvertent balloons—red, black, yellow; ribbed and unribbed, rolling around on the surface of the tank. "Hot dogs" we called them, and calloused was the recruit who couldn't at least chuckle at the sight, even after Powers Road.

We denigrated our job, making light of our low social status and cracking bitter jokes about how little our necessary and valuable role in the community was appreciated and commented upon. (We did, however, consider ourselves to be a couple of rungs above the garbagemen and the gravediggers.) But it was part of the *esprit de corps*—the laughter at our own expense that helped the shifts to pass. Unlike most of the public, we were keenly aware that the dramatic increase in human life expectancy in the developed world during the past one hundred years was due to simple sanitation—preventing diseases such as typhoid and cholera. The flashy, high-profile medical establishment is lauded for its progress, but no one has made a greater contribution to health, well-being, and longevity than the shitmen. If not for sewage plants, the cemeteries would still be filling with vast numbers of people whom we now consider to be young, fresh, and damn-near indestructible.

But it's a dirty job and people don't like to look. Even within the city administration itself, we were often poorly considered. The wage scale for a backhoe operator, a person who ran a relatively simple machine worth only $40,000 or so, was higher than the scale for a sewage plant operator, a person who ran a multi-million-dollar plant of intricate complexity. A person can learn to run a backhoe in a couple of hours (though it takes much longer to get *good*), but it takes a week to learn the *basics* of plant operation and several months before becoming a full-fledged, entirely competent operator.

Still, we were shitmen, and we stunk. During the July Fourth parade we would see the glamorous firemen, sitting proudly astride their great and shiny trucks, blue uniforms all spiffy as they tossed candy to awe-stricken kids. It was inspiring to us as well and gave us an idea for the ultimate sewage plant prank. We would clean up our sludge truck, hosing and buffing The Unit till it shone. We would have our coveralls dry-cleaned and order a case of brand new rubber gloves. Then, with a marching band in front and the firemen behind, we would proudly parade down main street on July Fourth. At the back of the truck we would mount a special platform upon which would be two full drums from the bar screen. As the crowd peered at us confusedly, muttering, "What the hell is that?" we would reach into the drums and pelt them with turds. "We're your shitmen!" we would shout as they all scattered for cover, learning anew what it meant to have raw sewage in the streets.

But of course it couldn't be. Our dramatic witnessing to the world would have to remain a relished fantasy. Our statements about what we had learned from handling the wastes of thousands of our fellows would continue in the form of personal jokes and pranks. Thus, in the enduring concrete of the sewage plant sidewalk can be read the inscription scratched in the cement by a plant operator: *En Feces Veritas.* It'll be there for decades—words for the salesmen, students, visitors, and for the ages (but mostly for the night shift): *In Shit There Is Truth.*

"I saw my evil day at hand."

Black Hawk

Mark Coyle

Seeing the Elephant

It's a perilous world. In the end there are no favorites—you're never too old or too young to die. But there are categories of danger. Some threats are flashy and grandiose, like skydiving or white water running, and are therefore purposely sought out. Other risks are just as dramatic but are fraught with routine anxiety, like firefighting or police work, and fall under the heading of "somebody's got to do it." Then there are the random, "accidental" dangers, like hurricanes or disease, which are not sought out but are endemic to the natural order.

These are all external perils, threats to the body. The mind responds and is affected, but it's not the *source* of the jeopardy. One of the most intimidating classes of danger is the menace that springs out of your own head. There's no particular time, place, or circumstance more conducive to this threat, but neither is there any guaranteed haven. It's pervasive, adumbral. For instance, I was once bullied in the mountains—by the Elephant.

I was a kid, a fledgling human unaccustomed to being alone and at the mercy of my untried mind, when I first saw the Elephant. I met it on a mountain trail, high above the timberline and miles into the wilderness. It was early morning, and I had just passed several restless hours in my tent as a solitary being in the black midst of a backwoods night.

I was planning to spend five days in the Rockies—backpacking, taking photos, communing with nature. But on the morning of that second day, I walked less than a mile, then stopped. Ahead, I could see the trail snake off into the distance, disappearing over the crest of a jagged ridge. The sky was vast—notched with snow-capped peaks—an overhead abyss. Below, a dark forest filled the valleys— an awesome outland of dense pine riding up the flanks of the mountains, the range of elk and bear.

Suddenly I felt small. Too small. Even if I had shouted or screamed, my voice would be lost, sucked up by the infinite sky— which didn't care. I tried turning to an imaginary companion, but the ancient rocks wouldn't allow it; my very thoughts were muted by their overbearing silence. The wilderness didn't need me, didn't want me. I was mortal, green, and far too new. I took one look at the face of the Elephant, then turned and hiked directly back to civilization.

The Elephant. It's a curious expression that comes out of the American West in the days of the expanding frontier. One chronicler of the era, Archer Butler Hulbert, wrote about a stretch of the California Trail: "Here we begin to meet people who are turning back, discouraged. They had seen enough of 'the Elephant.' No one seems able to explain that expression. . . . As applied to our case it means undergoing the hardships and privations of the California trip, and getting there. You hear the phrase used variously of these quitters that are heading back for Independence as: 'They've seen too much of the Elephant.'"

I imagined at the time of my failure that I had turned back because I was lonely and because I had never been in the mountains before. That was only part of it. I subsequently made solo trips that didn't disturb me—and journeyed through nearby, familiar forests only to find the Elephant there as well. Years after I'd first been flushed out of the mountains, I told the story of my aborted trip to an older man with much experience in wilderness travel. When I finished, he nodded, gave me a knowing smile and said, "Ah, you saw the Elephant."

"Yes!" I replied, excited about a shared revelation and suddenly bonded to a fellow traveler who understood. The Elephant is about limits: the limits of endurance, of weather and climate, of time and distance, of terrain, and of the mind's resilience. I learned that I had only glimpsed it on my mountain trip. Then I was inexperienced and timid, easily run off. But as I ventured on longer, more rugged forays into the bush, I penetrated deeper into the realm of the beast. I grasped that nature is a neutral force, powerful and aloof. However, humans like to think nature's relationship to us is much more personal. We like to think we're special individuals. Nature should love us; after all, we love nature, right? But to encounter the Elephant is to see that our love is unrequited. It is to be threatened, not just physically, but psychically. The Elephant is fear—of the unknown, of the dark, of emptiness, of death.

There is, however, another journey that I also vividly recall. My friend Mick and I were trekking through a vast stretch of Northern Minnesota wilderness. The first day was idyllic. We hiked twelve lazy miles in the early May sunshine with gentle light filtering through aromatic pines. The trail was rough and laced with tangled roots, but the vistas from the high ridges were splendid. We could see for miles over lakes and forests, a dramatic landscape carved by ancient glaciers. We dropped our packs several times to gaze, chat and doze, and we also camped early, pitching our tent beside a small waterfall. After supper we ascended a nearby escarpment to lounge on warm rock and await sunset.

But before the westering sun could paint the lakes below, a dark band of ominous clouds rolled in from the northwest. The horizon went murky; the sun was engulfed. Night came quickly, and we retreated to our sleeping bags.

The first drops of rain spattered the tent just before dawn. In a light drizzle we kindled a fire and heated a quick breakfast. We could hear wind advancing from a long way off, a steadily rising roar, like an approaching train. Soon the trees were swaying, lashed by cold arctic air. By the time we hit the trail, thunder and lightning were creasing the sky like an artillery barrage. We counted seconds between blasts and flashes, and the interval decreased rapidly. One tremendous thunderclap shook the ground under our feet, and somewhere off to the right a tree cracked. Then the rain was unleashed. It fell in wind-whipped torrents, heavy and icy-cold. The world went gray; the summery day before seemed like a fantasy.

After an hour or so we entered a swamp. It was low and sheltered, and the snow of the past winter still lingered, condensed into a slushy ice pack. For over a mile, as the rain continued to pour, we trudged over this cold sponge, occasionally breaking through into knee-deep freezing water. Despite our rain gear, we were soon soaked to the skin. The trees, brush, and ground were dripping and clammy. The rocks and roots were slippery and treacherous, the low areas now black quagmires of mud. The temperature had dropped to the low forties, with the wind chill effectively lowering it much further. Whenever we stopped to rest, we shivered, our teeth chattering—an early sign of hypothermia. There was no indication that the weather was going to improve, so we pushed on. Cold, wet, and afraid of the forces pummeling us from above, we struggled completely on our own, along the only track through a giant, wild land. Distance was against us, and the wind seemed alive and cruel; the sky was our enemy. This was how people died in the woods. We were seeing the Elephant.

At one point, after almost nine hours and only fourteen miles, the furious rain and gusts eased a little, and we paused, crouching on the spine of a thickly-wooded ridge. I was bent over, resting my soggy shoulders without dropping my pack, when Mick said, "Look."

I followed his gaze down the hillside. A ghostly mist was rising in the woods. The pine trunks, black with wetness, stood in dense serenity. My eyes could trail them, tree after tree into the distance, until the forest became opaque. The white fog, filmy and gentle, spread through the dripping branches and reached to the leaden sky. It closed us into the forest, leaving us surrounded by tall timber that seemed to sprawl forever.

Unexpectedly, verses sprang into my head, and I spoke them aloud:

"The woods are lovely, dark, and deep. . . ."

And how inviting it looked—to just drop my pack and wander off among the trees, not caring about rain or cold, not worrying about wetness, dryness, or how far out we were. How pleasant it would be to let go, to stop fretting about life and death, to roam the misty woods until struggle and pain lost all meaning. What was the worst that could happen? Yes, *that*, of course . . . but was that all? How strangely comforting to stare at the Elephant.

"But I have promises to keep. . . ."

I realized that, at least for the moment, I was no longer afraid. I had not become warmer or dryer or less tired. I hadn't grown stronger, faster, or smarter. I just was no longer threatened. I had the will to go on.

"And miles to go before I sleep."

There may indeed come a time when I'll wander off into the woods and never return. It'll be a fine day, but not yet.

Mick smiled at the recitation of Robert Frost, and soon thereafter we pushed on. Within minutes the rain resumed in earnest. So what? I was at peace with the fact that there was nothing I could do about it. I had seen through the Elephant.

*"Uncontrollable laughter arose
among the blessed gods."*

Homer

Patrick Dwyer

Last Laugh

I hope I still have "miles to go before I sleep," but I'm aware that glimpses of the Elephant are nearer at hand than a remote wilderness trail and that journeys often come to abrupt, unexpected conclusions. Such was the case with a boyhood friend named John Niemi.

I don't remember what the weather was the day we carried John to his grave in 1975. I have an impression that it was overcast, but perhaps it was my mind that was dark, and not the sky. It was autumn, so the maples must have been pretty.

I do remember the casket—I had never handled one before. It was bronze with gold handles, and very heavy. I gripped it tightly, forearm tensed, shoulder hard. I was horrified to think of dropping it. But that wouldn't have been the worst thing to have happened that day.

The episode began in northern Manitoba a few days before. John and Brian were hunting moose, and Brian shot John in the chest with a .30-06. I never got it straight how the mishap occured—the various reports juggled the details. Had the moose come between them, with John being hit by a stray bullet, or had he been directly mistaken for the quarry and purposely shot? In any case, he had had time to gasp, "Jesus Christ, I'm hit!" He was twenty-three.

Ironically, only a few weeks earlier, John had attended the funeral of a cousin and subsequently told his foster father that there was no way he wanted a conventional, impersonal funeral when he died. He wanted at least one of his friends to say a few words to temper the official sterility of it all.

So Doc asked me if I would. He was taking it hard. John had been orphaned at age fifteen, and Doc had taken him in. They had quickly become friends, as close as, or perhaps closer than, a real father and son. They even looked alike. Doc wanted me to speak at the services, and I was panic-stricken. What to say? What in the world *could* be said? But it was impossible to refuse.

The next day I received two telephone calls—one from the funeral director and the other from the minister who would preside at the service. They both wanted to cancel my eulogy. They were worried that I was going to make people feel worse, and, of course, I would definitely upset the sacerdotal routine. They didn't know I had been wavering, and if they had left me alone I might have backed out anyway. But their tones of condescension—"Are you *sure* you want to do this?"—made me angry, and *sure*. I agonized for hours over a speech that would require three minutes to deliver. And it almost didn't happen.

The organ music was deadly. As we all filed past the open casket, staring at the frozen, entropic features of death, the organ moaned softly in the background. The melodies were nondescript—mournful patterns of low notes. In isolation the music might have been beautiful, but in the context of coffin and corpse it was morbid, reeking of impotent platitudes. As the minister stood to speak, the funeral director approached the casket. The organ suddenly rose in volume, like a drum roll. As the undertaker closed the lid, the music reached a wailing crescendo, and we heard the loud "click" of the coffin lid locking. Then cut! The organ ceased. There was a communal gasp of dismay. People who had stopped crying started again. I shook my head, stunned. The minister spoke.

This man in black was a stranger. John had darkened the door of a church once in the past ten years, and that had been for his mother's funeral. The minister really had no place there, but he opened his book anyway. It was a black loose-leaf binder—a standard funeral spiel to get him through the motions. It's a job.

The sermon was also nondescript. The only thing I remember was the mention of Ernest Hemingway's suicide. I was at a loss to make a connection, except that he had been one of John's favorite authors. The man in black didn't know this. His words drifted over the muted sobs and quiet sniffling—unaffected, unaffecting. The sounds were joyless, devoid of hope. I concluded that the man shouldn't be allowed near a funeral. Unless, of course, it was his own.

I assumed that I would speak immediately after him and prepared to rise and stride to the podium. But as soon as the last syllable was uttered, the funeral director materialized at the side of the casket and beckoned for the pallbearers. His assistant had already opened a door to the outside. They had aced me out! Whether by accident or design, my eulogy had been shunted aside. But perhaps they planned for me to speak at the graveside; surely that was it.

With the casket safely inside the hearse, the pallbearers squeezed into a limousine and started for the cemetery. It was a two-mile drive, and the first half was endured in cold silence—all of us numbed by the preceding service. But as we approached the final turn off the highway, the mood broke. The same road led to both the cemetery and the garbage dump, the landfill being about a half-mile beyond the graveyard. Charlie, the youngest in our group, dipped into some reservoir of courage (or wisdom) and said: "Hey! Let's take him to the dump!"

We exploded into uproarious laughter. Great idea! It was a comment John would've appreciated. I could picture him laughing. The tension in the car evaporated, and we all talked at once, relieved of the desperate duty of grief. George, an older man and a member of the state legislature, asked us to imagine the look on the funeral director's face as we cruised by the grave, grinning and waving, and then burned rubber as we split for the dump. We could have the casket lashed to the roof of the car, like a fancy, gilded canoe. The minister's black binder could be sent on ahead.

We barely had time to compose ourselves before we reluctantly led the procession into the cemetery. Some in the crowd may even have wondered at a stifled grin or two as we pulled the coffin out of the hearse and carried it to the hole. I looked around for the funeral director. Would I speak now? I jockeyed for position near the grave, but another minister was there, one who'd known John's mother. He stepped up and took charge. As we all huddled around on the damp grass, he read a short prayer. He sprinkled ashes on the lid of the casket in the form of a cross and then stepped away.

Now? The funeral director had his back to me, turning to speak to someone else. The minister was closing his prayer book and preparing to leave. A couple of people started to fidget, shuffle and walk away. No one beckoned or nodded to me. I was on my own, officially ignored. For a moment I was undecided. Here was a chance to fade away. The few who knew I was supposed to speak would soon forget.

But it shouldn't end like this. I couldn't allow grief and despair free rein. The men in black would not shove me aside. I strode to the head of the casket and cleared my throat. Instantly I had all the eyes.

My fear had been tempered by laughter, my tongue lubricated by anger. I had rehearsed the words so many times that there was little chance of tripping over them. But now I saw the challenge was not merely to speak, but to smile. I roved the faces before me, focusing on pairs of eyes. I began with an anecdote about John.

I told how at 150 pounds dripping wet, he had nevertheless had the spunk to be the center of our high school football team. Every game he had to block guys who outweighed him by 50-100 pounds— zealous young bucks anxious to drive through him or over him to get into our backfield. And before they tried, he had to deliver a smooth, crisp snap to the quarterback, concentrating not on the impending mayhem, but on the hike. He had to take care of the ball before he took care of himself. He was operating on a plane above the rest of the linemen, initiated into a higher degree of mental and physical control.

And he had one other responsibility. After each play, after he had invariably wound up in a violent, punishing tangle at the line of scrimmage, he had to leap up, trot into the backfield and raise his arms. As center, our huddle formed around him. He reorganized the team, efficiently knitting us together for the next play.

As right guard, I played next to John on the line, and we often ended up in the same mass of bodies, fighting together. I recalled one game when we were being badly beaten—outclassed in every way. We were taking an especially severe hammering on the line. Late in the fourth quarter, after yet another punishing running play, I was slow in getting up. I was tired, sore, and feeling a little self-pity. I wearily lifted my faceguard out of the dirt and looked up. There was John, already up and in the backfield. His jersey was all askew, ripped out of his waistband and partially pulled down over a shoulder pad. His white pants were now black and green, smeared with dirt and grass stains. Twin streams of blood flowed from his nostrils down over his lips and dripped off his chin. The front of his jersey was red and wet, blotched with blood. There were drops on his shoes, and in the turf around his feet. But his arms were raised in the air. I jumped up. Though pummeled and battered, John was beckoning us to the huddle for yet another crushing play. The scoreboard was lit with 20-0, but it now seemed trivial. Seeing John, bloody and slightly bent with exhaustion, with his arms raised, I understood that on that day winning or losing had nothing to do with the score. I ran back to the huddle, re-fired. I slapped John's back. He almost smiled.

I had seen John's face for the last time today, I told the mourners, but the image from the huddle was the one I would remember.

It may have been wishful thinking, but didn't all the sad eyes light up? Just a little? I told them I didn't know what they believed as far as an afterlife was concerned, but as for me, it wasn't time to say good-bye, but only, "I'll see you, John." I patted the casket. Some of the ashes dribbled off. I walked back into the crowd. Doc caught my eye and whispered, "Thank you." No, I thought, thank *you.*

And now, as I finish this, I remember the sky *was* overcast. But I recall how the darkness abruptly left my mind. And yes, the maple leaves, though dead, were pretty. They'd be back in the spring.

"Let the woman into Paradise,
she'd bring her cow along."

Russian proverb

Mark Coyle

Midway Road

It was the spring of 1985 when I met the raggedy woman.

She was waving a pair of white gloves. As I drove by, I thought for a moment she was just being friendly—an old, bent crone, limping along the shoulder of the road, greeting motorists. But as soon as I passed her I realized that didn't make sense. I looked in the rear view mirror and saw she was trying to hitch a ride.

She was clothed in a long dress, black rubber boots, a dirty jacket and a white babushka. You'd guess just by looking that she didn't speak English very well. As three more cars passed, her waving seemed to grow more insistent, and she leaned a little farther out into the highway. I turned into a driveway, watching. Four more cars passed. Did I want to "get involved?" What if she was senile and lost? What if she was having some medical emergency and I couldn't understand her? What if she was just crazy? Six more cars ignored her, and I was ashamed. I turned out of the driveway and headed back up the road. She saw me coming and struggled across the highway, hobbling as if she hurt.

She was very old and weathered, probably European-born, perhaps Russian or Finnish. She opened the door and spoke rapidly in a heavy, unidentifiable accent.

"I been to town . . . paid taxes . . . I own land . . . I'm good woman!" she said, trying to impress upon me that she was no bum, no mere vagrant. She grinned as she labored to climb into the car, and her whole face wrinkled, a mass of lines and cracks. "You good man . . . I need ride . . . I pay!"

When she closed the door, the car was permeated with a foul odor, the smell of stale sweat and urine. I made an effort not to notice and said I was happy to give her a ride. Where did she need to go? She told me, and my fears were confirmed: I couldn't understand.

"Mitveyrut," she said.

"What?"

"Mitveyrut."

It made no sense at all, and I apologized, saying I didn't quite hear.

"Mitveyrut!" she said, louder, irritated by my denseness. She jabbed her finger east, and then it came to me—Midway Road. I heaved a sigh of relief.

"Midway Road?"

"Yah. Mitveyrut."

It was about eight miles away, and I learned she had left her farmhouse at 9:00 a.m. to make the trip to town. It was now 3:00 p.m., and she had walked a good portion of the distance, lugging a bulging plastic garbage bag. It appeared heavy, and I was amazed. She had to be in her eighties, and she didn't walk very well.

"I come pay taxes," she said, "but government . . . they took my boy . . . in war. Isn't it crazy?" Had to be World War II, I thought.

She talked nonstop. I learned that her husband was also long dead and that she lived alone on "lots land, have lots land . . . so much to do in country."

She asked me what I did, and I told her I worked at a sewage plant.

"Eh?"

"Sewage plant. Sewers."

"Ah, sewer. Yah, I know sewer . . . willow roots plug sewer, I scoop out . . . dangerous, be careful." She paused. "They took my boy . . . they took my boy." It was matter-of-fact, no tears, just resignation. She looked at me. "Isn't it crazy?"

"Yes."

In town she had also gone to a lumberyard looking for plywood for her floors. But the price she was quoted was too high. She swore energetically as she recalled the figure.

"You look like working man," she said. "Lots to do in country . . . I pay!"

We turned off the highway onto a dirt road, and she pointed to her farm. The fields were overgrown, untended, and the barn was lopsided with neglect, but her house looked sound and freshly painted. There was a low fence across the driveway; it had been a long time since a vehicle had been driven into the yard. She directed me to pull off to the side of the road.

"Thank you, thank you . . . you good man . . . I pay!"

I protested as she struggled out of the car, but she was forceful and adamant. I would be paid; she was no bum. I gave in. She had a right to pay, a right to dignity.

She stood outside the car and laid her plastic bag on the seat. Inside was a tattered purse, looking as ancient as herself. She reached inside and drew out a great wad of folded envelopes, worn and dirty. They were stuffed with money. She fumbled with one and pulled out two one-dollar bills. I thanked her.

"Welcome. If see me on road again, you give ride?"

"Sure."

Then she picked up a walking stick she'd left by the fence and, stepping over the barrier, trudged up the steep driveway. I waved as I drove off, but she didn't turn to look.

When I told Pam the story it made her sad; she said it was depressing. But I recalled the visits I had made to nursing homes. I remember vacant faces in front of TV sets. The rooms were comfortable and the people didn't stink, yet . . . I thought of one time in particular when I had met an old man named Cal. We had talked for a while, and more than once he had said, "I'm just waiting for Christ to come."

So what of the hitch-hiker? Sad? Yes, but only because we all age and die. I don't know how I'll be when I grow cracked and withered, what I'll think. As one young and healthy, dare I presume? Yet I know how I feel now. Will I want to sit and watch, waiting? Far better the hard road, limping and hiking and cursing the price of plywood. Christ will return in any case.

*"Jonathan made a scree of delight,
the first sound he had made
since he had left earth. 'IT WORKS!'"*

Richard Bach
"Jonathan Livingston Seagull"

Fred Yiran

Free Beer and Destiny

Some of my guests were timid at first. They couldn't get it into their heads that the drinks were *not* being tallied on my personal tab. They knew I couldn't afford this extravagance, and it made them nervous. I appreciated their neighborly concern, but for the third time I explained that this was free booze, paid for by an editor in distant, chimerical New York. Upon accepting my book manuscript for publication in early August 1986, the man had written: "If you want to treat everyone to a drink at either one or both of Side Lake's taverns, please do and send me the bill."

I informed my guests that Harper & Row had recently awarded David Stockman a $2,000,000+ advance, and the eminent publishing house could certainly afford to buy us backwoods folks a few Molson Canadians and Colorado Bulldogs. This class-conscious remark loosened up the conservatives and the bashful, and we drank toasts to my editor, Stockman, and anyone else who came to mind. The bartender kept track of our benevolence.

Surrounded by friends and well-wishers (some of whom would appear in *Letters from Side Lake*, my first book) and warmed by a couple of free beers, I indulged myself with pleasant thoughts of

175

predestination. Within five minutes of receiving the joyous news from Harper & Row, the acceptance had seemed unremarkable, natural. After the fact, any event—even an amazing one—seems inevitable. As we awaited another round, a friend shoved an illegal Cuban cigar into my hand, and that alien contraband seemed instantly familiar. Why not? For the moment I was a celebrity, a "fat cat," directing the liberal dispensation of free drinks to the house. It was appropriate to be brandishing such an ostentatious cigar. I don't smoke, but it's the thought that counts.

And there were so many thoughts; a full reckoning would have been impractical (actually impossible, given the fleeting nature of tavern meditation). Freshly annointed with success, most of my thoughts were sentimental. Snatches of nostalgic recollection briefly surfaced amid the intense partying of the present. A beer bottle makes a poor mirror but can be an excellent crystal ball. Occasionally the dark glass would conjure up an image from the past, a bench mark on the ineluctable path.

I remembered my paper route, taken on in 1964. It was my first tangible connection to the publishing world. (Actually the very first was a poem I had published in the local newspaper when I was in the second grade, but I was too young to appreciate the insignificance.) I handled sixty-four customers, and my canvas sack bulged—such a heavy burden of words and sentences. Paper and ink were weighty, substantial. Every day I passed out millions of words, and they seemed important to people. Customers were upset if I skipped them or if I ran a little late and they had to call to see what the hell had happened to their paper.

But I didn't miss a delivery often. After a year on the route it was hypnotic. My body slipped into autopilot, mechanically dumping the volatile news of the 1960s onto peaceful porches, as my mind wandered free. It was in the midst of this hypnosis one day, at age fourteen, that I decided I would be a writer. Maybe it was from hauling around so many words. Or maybe it was the short story I had just written for a junior high English class. I thought it was excellent, and it had come easily, so maybe I should be a writer. (I still have that story. I chanced across it the other day, and of course it's garbage.) In any case, I don't remember exactly why, but I do remember exactly where. Even today I could return to my hometown and show you the precise spot (within twenty feet) on the cracked sidewalk of Third Street N.W. where I was "overtaken by the muse." Perhaps someday, when I'm a famous and wealthy writer, the city fathers (who'll all be much younger than me by then) will see fit to install a commemorative plaque at that location. I could probably come up with a nifty dedication speech, something grand about fate and destiny. But I won't hold my breath.

As I resurfaced in the tavern, cradling an empty beer bottle/ time machine, I saw my friends John and Neil squared off over by the pool table. They were fencing with cue sticks, and it was obvious that one or both of them was drunk. It was a high school stunt, but that's what happens with free booze and a credible excuse to celebrate. It reminded me of other foolish, sophomoric activities and of a single word in my 1969 high school yearbook. The bartender brought a full crystal ball, and I remembered that prophecy.

Besides our senior mug shots, the yearbook contained a list of our respective high school affiliations and achievements, and in that section we were asked to note our "ambition." It was an assignment that cried out for creativity. Most of my classmates opted instead for honesty, offering "mechanic," "housewife," or the ever-popular "undecided." I wrote down "poet," and it duly appeared in black and white on the glossy page of the yearbook. I even meant it, a little. I had read that Ben Johnson, the third Poet Laureate of England (1619-1637), requested he be paid with a supply of dry white wine. He believed that sack was the proper wages for a poet. It sounded uncomplicated and romantic. I'd be a writer of verse, the next Robert Frost; or failing that, the next Bob Dylan. (Like him, I grew up in Northern Minnesota and don't have a good voice.) Strangely, no one made fun of my "ambition." It was apparently too weird for words. (Or maybe it had the ring of authenticity—after all, I'd been published in the second grade.)

At college I raced bravely into a detour. I majored in theology, caught up with lust for an ill-considered idealism. I gave up the potential dissolution and frustration of a writing career for the potential responsibility and frustration of the ministry. Though well-intentioned, it didn't work. I discovered I was a heretic. The atmosphere of organized religion was too thin—I couldn't breathe.

After college and other misadventures, I experimented with various jobs and locales and finally settled in as a sewage plant operator in a small town only six miles from my even smaller hometown. Holding a BA in theology/liberal arts, I didn't consider myself unqualified. In that noxious environment of crud and putrefaction, my writing blossomed. Not a writing career, just the writing. I worked a swing shift, twenty-one days on and seven off. It was brutal and demoralizing, and quite literally stank. But on the night shift, that graveyard of sanity, there was often little to do. And so between naps, I wrote. And wrote and wrote and wrote. There had to be a way to escape that waste water dungeon, and maybe writing, my long lost desire, would be it.

Years passed—hundreds of shifts and swings. Pam took a reporting job at a local newspaper and from there went on to magazine free-lancing, backed up financially by my sewage plant money (properly laundered of course). She met with some success and often talked about her various editors and what kind of material they were gunning for. I listened and realized I had stuff like that. I shipped some off to a regional magazine and they bought it. "O frabjous day!" With the sewage plant as my base of operations, I free-lanced part time for a year, and then Pam took a lucrative public relations position with a Fortune 500 firm.

A few years ago I read an article in one of the news weeklies about the profession of writing. They examined the income of the people who were considered full-time writers, from free-lancers to reporters to the heavyweights like Michener and Vonnegut, and they determined that the average wage for writers was about $4.50 per hour. The difference between the high and low ends of the scale was astronomical. It was recommended by one wag that if one wished to be a writer, one should marry someone who earned at least $26,000 per year. So, I had finally hit pay dirt. The week after Pam started her new job, I quit mine and began writing full time. For the first year—1985—my wage worked out to $2.93 per hour. Before expenses.

I resurfaced in the tavern. John was now at my table, asking a woman next to him what he should do with the rest of his life. "Whatever you tell me, I'll do it!" he insisted. She somberly urged him to "eat shit and bark at the moon." He promised. He had just finished constructing a fragile, tabletop castle out of empty glasses, and Neil was dismantling it before it could collapse and shower us with shrapnel. Luckily, he got to it in time.

Luckily. *Luck.* Yes; how was that related to the ineluctable? Had Pam's PR job been "in the cards"? Well, then so had her layoff only nine months later. The company ran into some hard times and trimmed personnel. She got the axe, and our gravy train derailed. As fate would have it, both of us were now full-time writers. Whoopee. $2.93 times two equals poverty.

But I had recently been awarded my own bimonthly column in one of the in-flight magazines. It wasn't enough to support us; however, one day an editor at Harper & Row was on the plane and saw one of my pieces. He wrote to ask if I would be interested in doing a book. I carefully considered the proposal for a tenth of a second. There followed a contract, a healthy advance, and the party. (Oh yes, and the production of the manuscript.) The advance was enough to keep us solvent for several months. The tab for the party came to $214.95.

I had a second book, *The Bear Guardian*, published in 1990, and I hope someday to end the story with a glib "and the rest, as you know, is history." But predetermined? Snort! Yes, I work hard. Yes, I sometimes write well. Yes, I have a few (very few) connections. But that acceptance letter was not the product of fate and predestination. From paper route to sewage plant to acceptance party was the doing of that fast friend of writers: luck, dumb luck. And it's not ineluctable.

"Emergency Stopping Only"

Interstate Highway sign

Mark Coyle

Buddha on the Road

Should I pass the night sleeping or driving? At age twenty-two it would have been automatic: hit the road, the long romantic highway. By the time I owned my first car, the lust for wheels was a fever— I was primed to drive the world; as long as the radio worked.

But a decade-and-a-half later, in 1989, I was beyond the grip of pure instinct—at least for driving. Jumping behind the wheel was no longer reflexive, as American as a freeway. My seventh car was not a "big bright green pleasure machine" but a compact, efficient, necessary evil. Drive all night? Perhaps, but there were considerations: the weather, lower back ache, drunks crossing the centerline. Was it prudent?

After all, I had just worked the entire day as a teacher and sage. I had been dispensing wisdom to students at the University of Wisconsin-LaCrosse, sharing what I know about creative writing. Scraped down to the true grit of applying words to paper, there's really not much to tell. The essence of my knowledge was fully tapped between 11:00 a.m. and 9:00 p.m. (with generous breaks for lunch and dinner). The main tactic of writing is to do it . . . and do it and do it. Creativity is like love and hope, I told them. If you want to be loved, then love.

If you need to be hopeful, then hope. If you want to be a writer, then write. It's as simple and inscrutable as that. My goal was to say it a hundred different ways without being flippant or boring. "The secret," I blabbed to intense faces, "is that there is no secret." That rings so wise that it verges on utter banality. I should probably quit saying it.

Truly, I should have quit saying anything by 8:15 p.m. and still had time to drive to Minneapolis before midnight. But being a hired sage is seductive, and I carried on past 9:00 until the English professor who was my host tactfully cut it off. Before I said my good-byes, fueled the car and found the way out of town, it was nearly 10:00. It's two and one-half hours from LaCrosse to the Twin Cities, and I would arrive much too late to drop in on friends. From Minneapolis to home is a long haul: 220 miles, another four hours plus.

I had been offered a bed in LaCrosse, and of course I could always check into a motel, but I was feeling the old lure of the highway. I resisted, a little. I knew my wife would think it was dumb. I was drained from a day of peddling wisdom, there was snow in the forecast, I faced an unfamiliar route, and there would be more whitetails on the road than normal because it was deer season and the hunters had them moving and jumpy. "It's not safe," she would have said, and I would have felt stupid defending such a whim, so I didn't phone her before I left.

Safety. That was an abstract concept in August 1973. As I left LaCrosse it came to mind—that summer on the logging crew in the Oregon Cascades. It was potent seasoning, fraught with hazard and rich in characters and new country. Twice I had nearly been killed, but I had also earned a pot full of cash. It was time to buy that first vehicle (overdue, I thought, at age twenty-two) and navigate across the nation to home—from the West Coast to Minnesota, through the desert, over the Rockies, across the plains, and into the forest. I was atremble with excitement to be On The Road. From the pioneers down through Kerouac and bikers and truckers, the cross-country trek has been molded into an American hadj, and I was eager to be a pilgrim.

I started by getting ripped off at the used car lot. I paid $620 for a 1966 Ford half-ton pickup with 122,222 miles. I was blinded by the lack of rust. True, the right front fender was a little crumpled and corroded, but, being a northerner, I was accustomed to seeing five-year-old cars rotting away from grill to taillights because of exposure to winter road salt. This seven-year-old truck looked solid, and, having lived in Texas for the past three years, I was enamored of the idea of a pickup truck. Gas mileage was not a concern. The Yom Kippur War and subsequent oil crisis and price hikes were a full two months in the future. My chief problem would turn out to be motor oil mileage.

I left Roseburg, Oregon, at 5:00 a.m. on August 12. I was alone in my own vehicle with 2,000 miles of highway sprawling off toward the sunrise. I set Lake Superior as my general destination, and imagined the inland sea as a blue mirage beyond the curve of the horizon. I was on an Oregon Trail heading east, traversing territory I had never seen. This, I believed, was freedom. Movies, television, and popular records had imbued me with the mythology of modern wanderlust. "Easy Rider," "Route 66," "King of the Road," and countless others had fostered an image of enchanted roadways spanning a land of rugged yet glamorous locales. There was danger and beauty, hardship and romance. It was nostalgia for the vanished frontier, a denial of the fact that the continent had been settled—the bison shot, the Indians herded, and a service station every thirty miles. Americans still yearn to trek and explore, but there's nowhere to go. Thus we fantasize about our asphalt trails, saddled to horsepower instead of horses. The aerodynamic new cars streak through their television advertisements on winding, picturesque back roads, seeming to offer the possibility of wilderness travel in a Corvette or Mercedes. My old truck was no mule, but it more closely fit the terrain.

I watched first light at Crater Lake National Park, transfixed in reverent awe as the escarpments flushed a vibrant rose that darkened to orange then brightened to gold. The silence was like the breath of God, and I whispered the name in gratitude. The park was closed; no other humans disturbed the air. I had driven around a barricade to get in, an act of outlawry in keeping with the "frontier" and freedom.

By late morning I was over 200 miles down the road, out in the badlands on US 20 near Cougar Butte. I felt strong. Then my oil warning light came on. It was the cocked eye of a mocking demon. I stared at the red glow and felt a sickening lump crystalize in my guts.

The dipstick was dry, but I had two quarts of Havoline behind the seat, and that carried me to the next town where it required two and one-half more quarts to fill. I had assumed the old 352 V-8 would burn some oil, but I never speculated it would compete with fuel consumption. I was getting roughly sixty miles to a quart of 10-40. I bought two cases, and every hour I would stop to add a quart. It was an excellent way to stay alert, and it offered the illusion of nurturing a finicky steed.

In late afternoon I pulled into Boise and got tangled up with some real trouble. My radio quit. Music and The Road are Siamese twins and despite the regular oil chores, I'd never stay awake all night without tunes and news. My radio was the siren of the highway—enticing, melodious, and drawing me on. After I had determined that the problem wasn't a blown fuse, I stuck my face under the dash to hunt for a short in the power supply or a faulty antenna connection. Nothing. Disgusted, I threw my screwdriver into the glove compartment and slammed the door. The radio came on. And so it was that during the night-long cruise across Idaho I would reach over each time the music died and slam the glove box hatch.

I reached Lima, Montana, at dawn, as indigo mountains were stained red. I'd been at the wheel for twenty-five hours and covered 925 miles. When the innkeeper had me sign the register, I required a full ten seconds to recall my name. The woman gave me a funny look but took my money just the same. I was in an altered state, goofy with exhaustion and suddenly struck lonely by the astounding width of the continent. I stumbled to a phone booth and called an ex-girlfriend in Kentucky—got her out of bed. I regretted my weakness the instant she answered. It was a short, awkward conversation, and I reconciled myself to distance thereafter. Still, the call had been valuable because the first thing she had said was, "Where *are* you?" I realized then that one of the authentic liberties of being on the road is that no one knows where you are. Ask any kind of fugitive—"on the road" means over the wall, over the hurt, over the hump, out of the rut . . . gone.

I slept until noon, then took on Montana. At Livingston I bought rope. A wind off the Rockies was juggling the Ford from centerline to shoulder, and I knotted some extra cinches over the plywood topping the cargo. Most of my possessions were in the box, along with a buddy's stereo system, packed and wrapped like a Pieta on tour. It occured to me that I could stop anywhere and, if there was work, stay. I had everything I needed in the truck, and it wasn't full. I was young and lean with a fat wallet. I could do almost anything I wanted. I pounded my fist on the dash, thrilled by the power and glory of life. Unfortunately these blows made the radio cut out, and I had to slam the glove box door three times to get the music back. It was a scary moment.

At Billings I saw a sign for the Custer Battlefield National Monument, and if it hadn't been dark I would have detoured to the Little Big Horn. For a couple of hours I was haunted by history, even a little depressed that the highway had advanced so far in so little time. The night was spooky, dark clouds scudding past faint stars, and each time I stopped to add oil the back of my white neck tingled, as if expecting an arrow. I could have believed in spirits then, and at one stop I heard a pack of coyotes far off in the hills, yelping and howling—I felt both skittish and exhilarated, like a hunted creature.

I hit the North Dakota line as the stars faded toward daybreak, and I slept for several hours in Dickinson. Then I rolled across Dakota with bands of thunderstorms, I-94 a shimmering river in the glare of lighting. Low clouds compressed the plains, and the highway seemed like a tunnel through wheat. At sundown the sky was a gun-metal blue-black until the sun broke beneath the trailing rim of the storm cell and suffused the roiling ether with firey orange. It was so overwhelming I had to pull over before I swerved off into the fields, distracted by almost palpable light.

I crossed the Red River into Minnesota shortly after midnight and at 3:00 a.m. stood at a wayside rest on the shore of Leech Lake, twenty miles wide. The sky had cleared, and constellations seemed to rise out of the water, surfacing where the hazy northern horizon welded lake and sky. I stretched my legs along the beach, inhaling deep draughts of fresh darkness. It smelled like lily pads and pine pitch, garnished with a hint of recent rain. It was narcotic, and I returned to the road energized and tingling, counting deer and seeing their eyes as sparks of living voltage.

I wheeled into my mother's yard at dawn on August 15. I hadn't been home for nearly two years, but the past seventy-two hours out of Roseburg seemed like the bulk of my time away. Even at something less than light speed, travel had dilated time.

Even sixteen years later that trip loomed large in my memory. It had been a three-day meditation on wheels. Other than brief exchanges with waitresses and gas station attendants, I had spoken to no one. I was essentially sanctified—isolated as effectively as if I had been off in a cloister. Sure, I met a thousand other vehicles, but not their drivers; we were each inside a steel carapace, sealed behind gasketed doors and weather-stripped windows. At night I saw only headlights, flashing past and gone like a blink of basilisk eyes. I had greeted my mother, but it was difficult to speak—due partly to weariness but also to a strange reluctance to break silence, as if this highway anabasis had driven me not only to Minnesota, but to a vow.

After awakening from a long, still sleep in my childhood bed, I felt groggy and half-dead, hung over from a 2,000-mile binge. As I unpacked my truck at the curb, it was diminished—as if returned to a sales lot or consigned to a junkyard. It bore no outward indication of having traversed the West, spanning thirty degrees of longitude. A Conestoga or a horse would have shown signs of wear and trial, but I had only an odometer reading as evidence of passage (and two dozen empty oil cans). On the high plains the old Ford had been my vessel—sturdy, venerable, and a perfect match to lonesome highways. But on the residential streets of home, parked in the neighborhood of sleek, newer cars, it looked like the half-broken, oil-wasting, doomed wreck that it surely was. A few winters in Minnesota and cancerous rust would gut its body, assuming its V-8 heart lasted that long.

It had been a wonderful, sensuous ride, a youthful daydream fulfilled, but I realized as I lifted the stereo out of the box that there was no tangible way to tell it. Even the fragile turntable and speakers were unchanged. A damaged component would have been at least a token. I was thousands of miles from where I had been, so obviously I had moved—but what of the movement? Where had the miles gone? The vivid impressions of desert and mountains? The sense of the West? Perhaps I would have been thrilled by an arrow in the neck—or at least in a tire. I had expected to be transformed some- how by the journey. It was a pilgrimage, not to a shrine, but through the holy past to the present myths—Manifest Destiny to carefree highways. I had been homeward bound like a rolling stone and free as the wind blows, but I still felt like me. Shouldn't a journey so cele- brated and sung about have more effect? When and where were the coronations for kings of the road?

That evening I jotted down details of the trip, even composed a poem. I didn't want to forget the images. I was old enough to realize, of course, that there was always a letdown after excitement, that our lives simply won't hang in high gear but kick out of overdrive like the stick on a faulty transmission. But this had not been some frenzied Christmas morning where delight was blunted then extin- guished in an inverse square ratio with the ashes of anticipation. ("Is that all there is?") This had been the pilgrimage of a young adult, flushed with worldly success (after a fashion) and male prowess, enraptured by a cultural yen—by a human yen: The Road (or the trail, the river, the mountain pass), the Other Place, the unknown. Why didn't I feel different after such a trip? The obvious answer, not grasped until long afterwards, was: because I wasn't different.

The overriding fact of our existence is just *that*: our physical existence—with all its daily needs and wants. Transcendence is so intertwined with necessary routine that sometimes it's difficult to tell the difference between worry and worship. To paraphrase the sages: Prior to being enlightened, a person awakens in the morning, goes to work, comes home to eat dinner and goes to bed. However, after being enlightened, a person awakens in the morning, goes to work, comes home to eat dinner and goes to bed. The secret, as I had earnestly told my writing students, is that there is no secret. But that's not to say there is no mystery.

As I prepared to leave LaCrosse and drive all night, I hearkened back sixteen years to that trek across the West. What was mysterious to me at first was why I wanted to endure this mini-version of that old run. I knew it would be punishing, that after I slept and awoke the next afternoon I would feel terrible, that it would be mostly boring (unless I had an accident), and that my wife was right—it was dumb. There would certainly be little chance of enlightenment. Unless . . . unless somewhere out on the road I met the Buddha.

During my lecture about "no secret," I had illustrated my point by mentioning that an old warning of Zen masters to their disciples was: "If you meet the Buddha on the road, kill him!" I wondered why the master didn't say: "If you meet the Buddha in the temple . . . or in a hermit's cell, or at a garden shrine." Why, apparently, are you more likely to meet the Buddha on the road? You would "kill" him, of course, because his presence could only distract and weaken you. As Sheldon Kopp, "psychotherapist, guru, and pilgrim" has written: "The Buddhahood of each of us has already been obtained. We need only recognize it. Philosophy, religion, patriotism, all are empty idols. The only meaning in our lives is what we each bring to them. Killing the Buddha . . . means destroying the hope that anything outside ourselves can be our master." Or, if you prefer the Judeo-Christian version: ". . . work out your own salvation with fear and trembling." (Phil. 2:12)

But why *on the road*? Because, I learned, after much trial, error, and religious questing, that the road—that is, the streets, the alleys, the furrowed fields, the corridors, the assembly lines—is where true sages hang out. It's where people live, where the action is, where enlightenment bumps into paychecks and bowel movements. Not for nothing did the Beatles sing, "Why don't we do it in the road." That's where we do most everything—perpetual pilgrims.

As I drove across the Mississippi River bridge from Wisconsin to Minnesota, rolling down an exit ramp onto an unfamiliar highway that was nevertheless an old acquaintance, I chuckled to myself about that lecture. I must have sounded quite hip and "new age" to those students. But the Zen references had been spontaneous and thus may have even sounded sincere and wise. I didn't know if the students had gotten the point, but thinking of murdering the Buddha had certainly cleared my mind. He *was* on the road, there in my memory, and the mystery of this present journey evaporated: I was going to drive all night because it was better than sleeping all night. Simple fact. "Man, you gotta go," Thom Gunn introduced his most famous poem; he ended with, "One is always nearer by not keeping still."

And so I went, thrilling to the lights of Minneapolis-St. Paul, seen from a rise at midnight like a galaxy sprung out of the river, and shooting past them toward the soothing blackness of the Northwoods. And during the night I remembered the poem I'd written about my great passage across the West.

Eventually I'd realized that though the traveling itself hadn't changed me, there had been real value in what I made of the traveling. More important than the miles and images was what I had written about the miles and images. If you're going to write, I had told the students, then you must remember—as much as possible. I had stressed the utility of keeping a journal, of jotting down the de-

tails. And the night after the morning I had arrived home from
Oregon, I had written that poem. The title was taken from a freeway
sign: "Emergency Stopping Only." It's lousy verse, but still . . . To scan
it now is for me to feel as I felt on the road in August 1973, and that
is so precious it hurts. It's the only way back, and I must remember.

In traveling, writing, living, it all boils down to this: "If you meet
the Buddha on the road . . ." take notes. And then kill him.

The Author:
Peter Leschak has worked as a freelance writer since 1984. His work has appeared in such national periodicals as *Harper's, The New York Times Book Review, The New York Times Magazine, New Age Journal, Outside, Outdoor Life, Country Journal, Fine Gardening, Writer's Digest, Astronomy, Backpacker, The Photo District News, Children's Magic Window,* and *TWA Ambassador Magazine* (he was a columnist and contributing editor there 1985-86). A Minnesota author, Leschak has been represented in such regional periodicals as *Minnesota Monthly, Twin Cities* magazine, *Mpls/St. Paul* magazine, *Minneapolis Star & Tribune Sunday Magazine, St. Paul Pioneer Press/Dispatch, The Boundary Waters Journal, The New North Times, Lake Superior Magazine, Minnesota Fire Chief* magazine, *The Minnesota Volunteer, The Twin Cities Reader,* and the Hibbing *Daily Tribune.* His first book, *Letters from Side Lake,* was published by Harper & Row in 1987, with a trade paperback edition released in 1988.

Leschak's previous book with North Star Press of St. Cloud, Inc., *The Bear Guardian,* won the 1991 Minnesota Book Award in the nature category.

The Illustrators:
Bumming with the Furies is the third book **Mark Coyle** has illustrated for North Star Press of St. Cloud, Inc. Mark works as a freelance illustrator, is represented by Gray Gallery and teaches drawing to middle school children.

Patrick Dwyer homesteads in Collegeville Township and home-schools his three sons—Kieran, Emerson, and Liam—with his best friend, Jeanne. The arts are key to his daily routine and find many forms of expression.

Fred Yiran came from Cameroon, West Africa, had produced murals in Cameroon churches and schools, illustrated books for African writers and holds the following degrees in Fine Arts: BFA, MA in Studio Arts and Art History in African Arts. He is currently teaching school children in African arts and culture under the Central Minnesota Arts Board.